Powerful Principles
of Increase

Powerful Principles of Increase

by
John Avanzini

HARRISON HOUSE
Tulsa, Oklahoma

Powerful Principles of Increase
ISBN 0-89274-579-7
Copyright © 1989 by John F. Avanzini
Box 1057
Hurst, Texas 76053

Contents

Section III: God — the Greatest Giver!

Section IV: Ten Truths About Money

Section V: Five Major Mistakes About Money

This book is lovingly dedicated to
Patricia Ann Avanzini,
my partner in ministry and in life.

Introduction

What a wonderful experience you are going to have as you begin to experience *a transformation process in your mind!*

Keep this in mind: your new mentality will not come immediately. Oh, I know that in this "instant" society we have come to expect instant answers. Even Quaker makes instant oatmeal!

But, no one has invented an instant way to cause you to become a prosperous Christian. Your mental transformation process must occur in a biblical progression.

> **For precept must be upon precept, precept upon precept; line upon line, line upon line; here a little, and there a little.**
>
> **Isaiah 28:10**

This is exactly how God's prosperity mentality will transform your mind — concept by concept, precept upon precept, line upon line, here a little, there a little.

As you read the challenging concepts contained in the lessons in this book, you may question some of them. They may seem so dramatic, and so different from your present beliefs that you may question whether or not they are really biblical.

Well, there is a special scripture just for that questioning feeling. Let it be your guide as you undertake this thought-jarring, life-transforming experience:

> **To the law and to the testimony:** *if they speak not according to this word, it is because there is no light in them.*
>
> Isaiah 8:20

Go ahead and question the new thoughts I submit to you. Double-check the scriptures I quote in this book. Study their contexts. If this is to be a life-changing experience for you, you must *participate in the process.*

1. Read.

2. Question.

3. Research.

4. *Then* change.

Always remember that when dealing with God's mind on any matter, it is very common for His precepts and conclusions to be very different from our own. God puts us on notice of this possibility:

> **Let the wicked forsake his way, and the unrighteous man his thoughts: and let him return unto the Lord, and he will have mercy upon him; and to our God, for he will abundantly pardon.**
>
> **For my thoughts are not your thoughts, neither are your ways my ways, saith the Lord.**
>
> **For as the heavens are higher than the earth, so are my ways higher than your ways, and my thoughts than your thoughts.**
>
> Isaiah 55:7-9

Here is your challenge: *the concepts in God's Word are sometimes going to be very different from the current concepts in your mind.* Why? Because your mind has certain unscriptural concepts programmed into it, and those programs have been reinforced daily, and gone virtually unchallenged for many years. Remember: they were put into your mind precept upon precept, line upon line, here a little, there a little.

Therefore, they must be removed the very same way.

That is why God led me to create this book as a living tool to be used by the Holy Spirit, lesson upon lesson, to lead you into a new breakthrough mentality in your finances.

Remember: as you read these lessons, it is not enough to just put new information into your mind. You must get the old, erroneous, non-scriptural information you have stored up out of your mind forever. This false information came from many well-meaning people. Some of your concepts came from your parents, some from your teachers and some from pastors, preachers and Sunday school teachers. Some of your concepts came from the music you enjoy.

But, wherever your concepts came from, realize now that virtually every place you go, and in everything you experience, concepts and ideas are instilled in you — some are scriptural, some are not. You must now begin to regulate the input of concepts into your mind by feeding it only good Bible concepts regularly.

As you *participate* in this mind transformation, please do not hesitate to accept these new concepts just because they may not agree with what you have already learned over the years.

Just make sure that these concepts agree with the criterion of the Word of God!

Freely question and examine the concepts in this book; be absolutely sure they agree with Scripture. Then accept them and begin to put them into practice.

Let me make you a promise. I will not give you any new concept without also giving you the Scripture reference to support it. Please note: if you will demand this same scriptural standard in every aspect of your life, you will experience a whole new mentality, not just in the realm of God's finances, but in virtually every area of your life. The result will be a total transformation in your health, happiness, sanctification, and other areas too numerous to mention.

If you will, from this day forward, insist that every concept you learn line up directly with God's Word, you will soon have a new mentality about the Second Coming of Jesus Christ, about consecration and dedication, and about how to be a good Christian parent!

If you strictly demand that the only things you allow to stick in your mind are those things that line up with the Word of God, you will find yourself not easily misguided by new doctrines which come from many sources around you. You will find yourself rising up out of your defeat or near-defeat, and moving into new bold adventures for your God.

> **Casting down imaginations, and every high thing that exalteth itself against the knowledge of God, and bringing into captivity every thought to the obedience of Christ.**
>
> **2 Corinthians 10:5**

Notice that the process outlined in this verse is precisely the one we follow in this book. We are to *cast down* any imaginations that are against the knowledge of God, and *bring into captivity* every thought unto the obedience of Christ.

It is time for you to become the dynamic, surging force God intended you to be when He redeemed you with His blood and the Word of truth!

If there is going to be transformation in any area of your life, your mind must first be cleansed of the unscriptural principles and be reprogrammed to line up with God's original intentions in His precious Word. As your mind is "renewed," you will become what God intended for you to be in the very beginning, when He planned for you to have victories and conquests as you serve Him.

Through this book, I believe God will transform your thinking in the area of finances, and direct you right back to that plan!

Remember: if there is going to be a change in your thinking in the area of prosperity, you will have to *participate in the process.*

Allow God to gradually break through your old concepts and your old ideas. You must be willing to allow God's plan for your divine prosperity to crowd out the devil's plan for your mediocrity, failure, and continual insufficiency.

Lay firm hold on this fact — *the battle is in your mind.*

You are what you think you are. God's Word tells us:

> *For as he* (a person) *thinketh in his heart, so is he....*
>
> **Proverbs 23:7**

When thoughts enter your mind, they soon become deeply imbedded in your God-given "computer." Once a concept becomes part of your thinking process, it will guide you like a silent homing device that always brings you to the same, predetermined conclusion.

For various reasons, you may have already reached a "predetermined conclusion" that Christians should be poor. If you do not allow the Scriptures and God's Spirit to break through your old thinking patterns, you will continue to come to the same old unscriptural conclusion you did before you read this book, and you will remain without enough of what you need.

Have you ever heard the expression, "set in concrete?" The longer concrete sits, the harder it gets. After five or ten years, it is much more difficult to break up a concrete slab than it was soon after it had first hardened. Time actually makes concrete harder to break.

Time does the same thing with the unscriptural, unchallenged concepts in your mind. The longer they sit, unquestioned and undisturbed, the harder they are to break. Remember: God does not want your false concepts to harden and strengthen their grip on you. His Word tells you to cast them down and to break unscriptural strongholds off your mind.

As you read this book, I believe God will bring a great, "concept-shattering" *breakthrough* in your life.

He wants to break those old concepts which are "set in concrete" in your mind, and put His mind into you. After all, Scripture encourages us to have the mind of Christ:

> **Let this mind be in you, which was also in Christ Jesus.**
>
> **Philippians 2:5**

Notice, the verse does not say that the mind of Christ will instantly pop into you at the time you are saved. The Word says "*Let* this mind be in you."

You must participate in the process!

God's Word also talks about being "transformed by the renewing" of your mind:

> **And be not conformed to this world: but be ye transformed by the renewing of your mind, that ye may prove what is that good, and acceptable, and perfect, will of God.**
>
> **Romans 12:2**

Notice, this verse does not say that you will receive an instant, Quaker-oatmeal type of transformation. It does say there are some new dynamic thoughts Jesus wants to put into your mind, and that those new thoughts will give you a new kind of life.

But, *you participate in the process!* Why does God want you to undergo this process? ...**that ye may prove** (literally, that you may have first-hand knowledge of) **what is that good, and acceptable, and perfect, will of God.**

As your bold new adventure begins, you will probably want to believe that God desires for you to "have the best," but you may be afraid. You may think:

"Oh, Brother John, I want this process to work so much. I want to believe in new, powerful, prosperous thoughts. I desire to have the abundance God speaks about in His precious Word, and to be able to freely give to the special projects God puts on my heart. I want to be able to travel to spiritually nurturing conventions. I want to support Christian television, mission endeavors, and many other powerful ministries. I'm tired of never-ending financial struggles; I want to be able to give generously to my church, and to my family."

You can do it!

But, you must first understand that everything runs in cycles. If you don't grasp this truth, you will miss everything that has to do with the abundance God wants to give to you.

To "run in a cycle" simply means to run in a circle — just like a dog chasing his own tail. The harder he tries to catch it, the more futile the chase seems. If you are now caught in the cycle of insufficiency, you will continue to "chase your tail" and come up with more and more insufficiency. You will not have enough to give properly, and in not giving enough, you will not receive enough. In not receiving, you will not have enough to give properly.

Somehow you must break out of that vicious cycle!

This is why God has led you to this book. As you accept the God-given truths you read here, under the influence of the Holy Spirit you will be led into a bold new cycle of abundance with God.

You see, until you become a great receiver, you will not be able to become a great giver; and until you become a great giver, you will not be a great receiver.

Something has to change. Something has to move. The insufficiency cycle has to be broken, and the abundance cycle must be started.

And the thing that has to move is that old thinking process that continues to bring you to the insufficiency you have lived with for so long. But now, let Jesus make all things new! God does want you to prosper! So from this moment on, lesson upon lesson, precept upon precept, let Him purge out the old concept of insufficiency and replace it with the new concept of abundance He has for you.

Once and for all, break the cycle of insufficiency!

Look at what the Apostle John "prays" in 3 John 2:

> *Beloved, I wish* (pray) *above all things that thou mayest prosper* and be in health, even as thy soul prospereth.

My, what a wonderful thing John prayed for you. He could have prayed that you would learn to live with shortage and insufficiency, or that you would learn to be content in your poverty. He could have prayed that you would have the ability to scrimp and scrape in your hour of need. But no, instead John speaks of a great, bold, powerful move in your life, a "God-kind" of move, the kind that would bring you...

- Out of the cycle of lack, and into the cycle of abundance...

- Out of the cycle of want, and into the cycle of more than enough.

Aren't you really tired of being continuously short of the material substance you need to fully and completely obey God in the many wonderful ways He wants you to give?

Now, before you begin this powerful, stirring process of prosperity breakthrough thinking, let me share with you a few, final thoughts.

God never gives you a vision that is larger than what your finances *would have been* (notice I didn't say *are*) at the time of your vision, if you had obeyed Him every time in the past when He had told you to give, and if you had always given the amount He said to give.

Your current financial condition is determined by your past obedience in giving.

Your future financial condition will be determined by your obedience today.

You see, you do not receive from God in accordance with your need.

Please do not run to Philippians 4:19 and begin to quote it to me: **But my God shall supply all your need according to his riches in glory by Christ Jesus.** That promise does not start in verse 19; it actually begins in verse 15, where Paul speaks to the Philippians who were mission givers. Because of their regular support of his ministry, Paul spoke this blessing upon them. The blessing of Philippians 4:19 is not the property of the whole church world. It applies only to those who regularly support world missions!

God is not moved by need. If He were, He would only bless the areas of the world where the need is greatest.

He would bless the starving in India.

He would send food and rain on portions of Africa, where men, women, and little children are dying by the tens of thousands amid severe drought and famine.

He would move only on skid row, and not in the highrise penthouses in the very same city.

But many times God moves in the most affluent situations. You see, as hard as it may seem for our old mentality to accept, God is not moved by need; God is moved by faith. The reason God is moved by faith is because true faith brings *obedience*.

Every time God tells you to give a certain amount, you must release the amount He tells you to give, whether it is given to your church, to a Christian telethon or to a great mission endeavor. God is not only raising money for the "vision" or outreach to which you are giving, He is also raising future money for you and for the vision He plans for you to accomplish for Him.

You see, God is teaching you the *process* of sowing so you can have an abundant harvest when you need it, so you can move into your special vision, and have your special need met.

If you start now, understand that there will be a little time of catching up to God's prosperity for your life. Remember: you did not get into your present situation in a day, so do not expect God to get you out of it in a day. We never reap the same day we sow. It will take a season for your new prosperity crops to become ready to harvest.

Remember: the Bible says that if you sow, in due season, *you will reap!*

If you cast your bread on the water, in a number of days, it will come back to you again; God says the blessings will overtake you!

God's Word is pregnant with promises of reaping the harvest if you are faithful in sowing.

So begin now. Make yourself a promise. Make your God a promise.

Each morning read one of the lessons in this book. Do not go to sleep in the evening without once again reading that same lesson. If you can, read the lesson a time or two again and meditate on it through the course of your day. Spaced repetition has been proven to be the most effective type of learning. Speak the concepts out loud, if possible, all day long, as often as you can. If you will dedicate yourself to this task, then the Word of God will begin to live in you in the realm of prosperity. Your new prosperity mentality will bring you "the riches of the Gentiles," (Is. 61:6, Rom. 11:12) and put into your hands the keys to the treasure house of God. You can learn to finance the end-time harvest God's way!

Let's keep the proper perspective. God doesn't want to prosper you so you can lavish it on yourself, as much of the current teaching tells us. However, God will prosper you so you can be a potent, effective force in *reaching the world for Jesus Christ* through your giving.

In fact, the Bible speaks of a ministry — a special grace for giving — so we can literally become "God's bankers," those who will finance God's work with the money with which He has prospered us.

Now don't get discouraged. God will bless you abundantly as you move into this mentality of abundance. God wants you to enjoy and "eat" from that which you bring forth. God said that a servant is worthy of his hire. He will see that you have more than enough.

> But remember this — if you give little, you will get little. A farmer who plants just a few seeds will get only a small crop, but if he plants much, he will reap much.
>
> Every one must make up his own mind as to how much he should give. Don't force anyone to give more than he really wants to, for cheerful givers are the ones God prizes....
>
> Yes, God will give you much so that you can give away much, and when we take your gifts to those who need them they will break out into thanksgiving and praise to God for your help.
>
> **2 Corinthians 9:6,7,11 TLB**

Keep this in mind: you cannot be God's banker with a poverty mentality. You cannot be God's banker if you are shy and ashamed and embarrassed about boldly taking a portion of the wealth and finances of the world and bringing it under your control. You cannot be God's banker unless you are convinced that God wants you to prosper — unless you know that His laws of prosperity can apply to your daily life.

You can break through in your financial situation if you will hear God clearly as He speaks to you from the pages of the Bible. I promise you that in this book you are about to read I will not give you my thoughts. I will only give you the thoughts of God which are clearly written in His Word.

So now, if you are ready, make this commitment. Please pray this prayer out loud:

"Dear God, I make a solemn commitment to You today. I promise You, Lord, that each day I will digest one of these lessons, and will allow Your wonderful truths to become a part of my life.

"Lord, I know that as I draw nigh to You, in this new mentality, You will draw nigh to me, even as the scripture says.

"O God, I thank You that I can come to You, knowing You are a covenant-making God. I now make this covenant with You, with the angels as a witness.

"Lord, I will be faithful in this covenant, and I know that You will, in Jesus' name, be faithful in Your promises to me. Amen."

My prayer, from the very beginning when I started writing this book, until now as you read it, has been that you will experience a new, prosperity mentality. I pray that your mind will be turned upside down by Jesus Christ through His precious Word, and that all your old concepts will be replaced by a fresh, new, God-given prosperity mentality.

One Final Note to the Reader

You will no doubt skim through the pages of this book before the designated day you read each daily lesson. Please do *not* let this stop you from reading one lesson each morning, and then rereading the lesson again that night. Without this precept-upon-precept, line-upon-line method of learning, the impression you feel in your mind will not be nearly as strong.

Also note that couples and families can read these lessons together, or they can be read in a daily Bible study at work, in the neighborhood, or at school. For best results, however, each person should have a copy of this book for notes and rereading each lesson in the morning and evening.

— John Avanzini

Section I:
Poverty or Prosperity?

Lesson 1: Poverty or Prosperity
— the Choice Is Yours!

Satan has lied to the saints! For too long the devil has told us this lie:

"Some people are destined to be poor, and some people are destined to be rich, and there's nothing anyone can do about either circumstance."

This satanic lie has crippled the finances of individual Christians and Christian ministries for far too long! It is time we learn the truth! There are three main reasons why this destructive statement is a lie:

1. *It is a lie* because God is not a respecter of persons.

> Then Peter opened his mouth, and said, Of a truth I perceive that God is no respecter of persons.
>
> **Acts 10:34**

God did not predetermine who would be rich and who would be poor. He simply created His spiritual laws, and freely gave them to everyone. Every person then has a choice — to implement the laws of poverty, or to implement God's spiritual laws of prosperity.

2. *It is a lie* because God's desire is that you prosper.

This truth is plainly stated in Scripture:

> *Beloved, I wish above all things that thou
> mayest prosper* and be in health, even as thy soul
> prospereth.
>
> 3 John 2

Prosperity, not poverty, is God's intention for your life.

3. *It is a lie* because God has given you the power to get wealth!

> But thou shalt *remember the Lord thy God:
> for it is he that giveth thee power to get wealth,*
> that he may establish his covenant which he sware
> unto thy fathers, as it is this day.
>
> Deuteronomy 8:18

God would not give you the power to get wealth if He did not intend for you to *use that power* and become wealthy! The decision to live in poverty or to live in prosperity is *yours!*

God has already cast His vote — *He wants you to be prosperous!* Make your life-changing decision today to reject the destructive laws of poverty and to accept your God-given rights under God's law of abundance.

Remember:

- God is no respecter of persons. (Acts 10:34.)

- God wants you to prosper. (3 John 2.)

- God gives you the power to get wealth. (Deut. 8:18.)

Lesson 2: The God-Given Laws of Poverty and Prosperity

God has created spiritual laws that determine who has wealth, and who will remain poor.

That's right!

The laws of poverty and the laws of wealth are authored by the same God Who created the law of gravity, and *all* of His laws work every single time they are applied.

An apple will always fall to the ground. That's God's law of gravity.

A person will become rich or poor — by following God's laws.

One of the *laws of poverty* simply says, "If you are lazy, or if you do not understand your task, then your fields will not bring forth abundance; they will only grow thorns and nettles (a symbol of the unproductive yield that brings about want and insufficiency)."

> I went by the field of the *slothful*, and by the vineyard of the man *void of understanding;*
>
> And, lo, it was all grown over with thorns, and nettles had covered the face thereof, and the stone wall thereof was broken down.
>
> Proverbs 24:30,31

One of God's *laws of prosperity* simply says: "If you are not lazy, and can work without supervision, you will receive a bountiful supply."

> Go to the ant, thou sluggard; consider her ways, and be wise:
>
> Which *having no guide, overseer, or ruler,*
>
> Provideth her meat in the summer, and gathereth her food in the harvest.
>
> Proverbs 6:6-8

Do you feel the old concepts in your mind starting to fall away? Right now you are probably saying, "But Brother John, I resent the implication that I'm lazy. I'm not, and yet I'm continuously without the abundance that I need."

Remember: I have only touched on two factors in a poverty mentality today — laziness, and the lack of proper understanding to perform a task. There are many other laws.

Just allow your *process of participation* to start. If you do not become "set in concrete," you will experience a gradual transformation of your thoughts into your prosperity mentality.

Do as the Bereans did in the first century: they received the Word readily, and searched the Scriptures daily to see if these things were so! (Acts 17:10-11.)

Lesson 3: God's Law of Reward

There are four "R's" which govern the laws of poverty and prosperity:

1. Reward   2. Release

3. Receiving   4. Reaping

First, I want you to think about *reward.* God's Spiritual Law of Reward simply states:

> **...for the labourer is worthy of his hire (reward)....**
>
> **Luke 10:7**

Your employer is not doing you any special favor by writing you out a paycheck. Whatever your vocation, your wages are yours — scripturally, morally, and legally! You earn them. They are not a gift.

When you work hard, God's law demands that you receive your reward!

> **He that tilleth** (works hard) **his land shall have plenty of bread....**
>
> **Proverbs 28:19**

If you are currently working hard, expect to receive your just reward.

Now there is another side to this Law of Reward!

No work = no reward.

God's Word is very emphatic about this:

> **But if any provide not for his own, and specially for those of his own house, he hath denied the faith, and is worse than an infidel.**
>
> **1 Timothy 5:8**

Again, in 2 Thessalonians 3:10 we are told:

> **...if any would not work, neither should he eat.**

Plant this law firmly into your mind. Like all of God's spiritual laws, it is an absolute! Those who "till" the land will have "plenty of bread." If your hard work is not bringing "plenty of bread" into your life right now, then some spiritual law of poverty is working to stop God's desire for your life.

Day by day, as you examine the different spiritual laws for prosperity, you will begin to understand that God's perfect will for your finances is for you to prosper and have more than enough.

Remember:

• The laborer is worthy of his hire. (Luke 10:7.)

• If you work hard, you will have plenty of bread. (Prov. 28:19.)

• Any person who won't provide for his own family is worse than an infidel (a non-believer). (1 Tim. 5:8.)

• The Bible says that if you won't work, you shouldn't eat. (2 Thess. 3:10.)

Lesson 4: God's Law of Release

Poverty is not an accident, and neither is prosperity! Strict spiritual laws govern both.

The second "R" for poverty or prosperity is *release*.

The Spiritual Law of Release concerning prosperity says: "Be willing to *release* for the increase!"

> **There is** *(he) that scattereth, and yet*
> *increaseth;* **and there is** *(he) that withholdeth more*
> *than is meet, but it tendeth to poverty.*
>
> **The liberal soul shall be made fat: and he**
> **that watereth shall be watered also himself.**
> **Proverbs 11:24,25**

I do not know any other place in Scripture where God makes it any clearer than here in Proverbs. Scatter your money, it will increase, and you will be prosperous; hoard too much of it, more than is fitting, and you will be poor!

God's spiritual law will not change, no matter how uncomfortable it makes you feel. Right now, you may be saying, "But, Brother John, you mean I have to start giving my money away if I want to be prosperous? That doesn't make any sense."

You are right. In the eyes of the world it does not make sense. One of your "old" concepts, "set in concrete," says: "Get all you can get, then keep the lid tight on the can." God's spiritual laws do not always make worldly sense, but they are His truths and will always work!

God's spiritual laws will not change. "Release, and increase (prosper); retain, and decrease (tend to poverty)!"

Remember:

• Prosperity is not an accident, and neither is poverty.

• Only when you decide to put God's spiritual law of release into action in your life can you expect God's promised law of increase to begin to operate for you too.

• God's law of receiving is clearly stated in Luke 6:38:

> Give, and it shall be given unto you; good measure, pressed down, and shaken together, and running over, shall men give into your bosom. For with the same measure that ye mete withal it shall be measured to you again.

Lesson 5: God's Law of Receiving

Remember the lame man at the gate called Beautiful? Acts 3:5 tells us that man was "expecting to receive something" from Peter and John before they brought him to his feet.

This man went away leaping and praising God!

Jesus must have walked by this man many times as he lay crippled at the gate. The man had never received before because he never expected to receive anything. However, when Peter and John came by, the man was "expecting to receive something of them," and he was healed! The only different ingredient was his anticipation!

Those who are expecting to receive something are the ones who will receive it.

Most of God's Word is illustrated with agricultural images — birds, fruit, planting, and harvest. Have you ever heard of a farmer who planted his precious seed and didn't expect a return?

Here is a shocker for you:

It is godly to give expecting to receive!

When God sent His Son, Jesus, to earth, the Father expected to receive something valuable in return — *sons* and *daughters!*

God gave, expecting a desired result; He gave, expecting to receive.

And Jesus, our eternal role model, was willing to give and to receive.

Once, when Jesus visited a Pharisee's house, He allowed a woman to wash His feet with expensive ointment. When His host criticized this woman, Jesus said, **...thou gavest me no water for my feet...but this woman hath anointed my feet with ointment** (Luke 7:44,46).

Jesus was a good receiver. Countless times in the Scriptures we see Him receive food, lodging, gifts and even the use of a donkey. Jesus freely gave, but He also was willing to freely receive!

When you do not follow in the footsteps of Jesus, or when you are not willing to be a good receiver, you stop the abundant blessings God wants to flow into your life.

Your failure to expect to receive from others will result in a subconscious resistance to receiving. Many times pride keeps us from receiving, but Proverbs 16:18 gives us strong warning about pride:

> **Pride goeth before destruction, and an haughty spirit before a fall.**

Do not let your false pride harden your mind and keep you from receiving from God, or from others. When Jesus said that it was more blessed to give than to receive, He didn't say we were not to receive.

Unless you begin to develop a receiving mentality, God cannot begin to bring prosperity into your life.

Remember:

• God gives, expecting to receive. He gave Jesus, expecting to receive you as a spiritual son or daughter.

• Jesus was a good receiver.

• Pride and a "hardened" mind will restrict and slow the flow of God's prosperity into your life.

Lesson 6: God's Law of Sowing

When a farmer puts a seed into the ground, he does not get back just one seed. When he puts that seed into the earth, a divinely ordered process begins. The seed produces a stalk of corn, the stalk produces several ears of corn, and each ear produces hundreds of new seeds — *all from the one seed the farmer planted!*

But, notice a very important point. The farmer has to *sow* the seed first before there can be a harvest.

And, the more seed he sows, the larger the harvest will be.

Remember 2 Corinthians 9:6,7 from *The Living Bible:*

> But remember this — if you give little, you will get little. *A farmer who plants just a few seeds will get only a small crop, but if he plants much, he will reap much. Every one must make up his own mind as to how much he should give....*

Then look at verse 10 of that passage:

> For God, who gives seed to the farmer to plant, and later on, good crops to harvest and eat, *will give you more and more seed* to plant and will make it grow so that you can give away more and more fruit from your harvest.

Every day you make a choice either to sow some of your seed, or to eat it. When you exercise faith and sow some of your seed, you release God's Law of Prosperity. When you give in to your fears — and eat your seed, or hide it — you release God's Law of Poverty.

Do not let your circumstances rule you. They may tell you that you can't afford to sow anything into the Gospel now. But Scripture clearly tells us that if we are ruled by our circumstances, we won't ever sow:

> He that observeth the wind shall not sow; and he that regardeth the clouds shall not reap.
> Ecclesiastes 11:4

If you do not sow, you cannot reap, but God's Word clearly tells you to sow in all circumstances!

> In the morning sow thy seed, and in the evening *withhold not thine hand:* for thou knowest

not whether shall prosper, either this or that, or
whether they both shall be alike good.

Ecclesiastes 11:6

Remember:

• Sow seed, and you will harvest. (2 Cor. 9:6.)

• When you sow, do not look to your circumstances. (Eccl. 11:4.)

• Sow regularly to every good work. (Eccl. 11:6.)

Lesson 7: God's Law of Reaping

The following statement is so simple it is deceptive. In actual practice, most saints do not believe it. If they did, they would all be enjoying God's prosperity in their lives:

If you sow, you will reap!

Repeat this statement out loud several times. Let it sink into your spirit: *"If I sow, I will reap."*

This is God's law; it cannot and will not fail!

God warns us not to be fooled or deceived:

Let him that is taught in the word communicate unto (share with) him that teacheth in all good things.

Be not deceived; God is not mocked: for whatsoever a man soweth, that shall he also reap.

For he that soweth to his flesh shall of the flesh reap corruption; but he that soweth to the Spirit shall of the Spirit reap life everlasting.

And let us not be weary in well doing; *for in due season we shall reap, if we faint not.*

Galatians 6:6-9

God's Spiritual Law of Prosperity says:

1. "Sow the seed."

2. "In due season, reap the harvest."

3. "What you sow is what you will reap."

As you sow your seeds into the Gospel of Jesus Christ, you will reap His harvest! God will take your seed and *multiply* it back to you.

Also notice the timing of the harvest. When will we reap?

"In due season."

So do not sow your seed one day, and expect to reap a harvest the next morning. Would a farmer plant his crops on Thursday, and then on Friday take his combine out into the field expecting to harvest?

Here's the final, vital point.

You will reap what you sow. "Whatsoever a man soweth, that shall he also reap." If you sow apples, you will reap apples. If you sow corn, you will reap corn. If you sow love, you will reap love. And, if you sow money, you will reap money.

Do not sow "good deeds," and expect God to return finances to you. Good deeds sown will bring back a harvest of good deeds!

God's spiritual law says if you sow good deeds, you will reap good deeds, not finances. If you desire more wealth and more money to meet your needs, then put more money into God's Kingdom. To reap a harvest of money, you must first sow money.

Even unsaved farmers know this principle, while many of the sons of God do not.

Remember:

• Farmers know that if they sow, they will reap.

• Farmers know they can reap only the kind of harvest they sow in the form of seed.

• Farmers know they cannot reap in the same season they sow.

Now do you see how important it is to know God's laws of the harvest?

Poverty or Prosperity?
In Summary

Can you feel your mind struggling to hang onto the old, comfortable concepts as you read this book each day? The startling statements in God's Word often shock and shake our old standard Christian concepts about poverty and prosperity.

Recognize the fact that your mind is now firmly engaged in the biblical process of transformation — precept upon precept, line upon line, here a little, there a little. Now your mind is starting to challenge and weed out the unscriptural, unfounded concepts, and is replacing them with sound, biblical truths. These truths will be able to set you free from want and insufficiency, and release God's abundance to you.

By now, I am sure you realize that this book, will challenge and transform your thinking in the area of God's abundant supply. Please continue to participate in the process as you read each day.

Do not try to find any quick, instant solutions in this book, but continue to use this proven biblical method. Take one lesson per day, read it in the morning, and then read it again in the evening. Give the new thoughts and ideas from each lesson time to become imbedded in your mind.

You are now on your way to breaking through your cycle of lack. You are on your way into the cycle of abundance and prosperity!

Just look at the startling progress you have already made in only the first seven lessons of your journey to a new prosperity mentality, and yet there are eighty-three even more powerful concepts that soon will be yours!

Now let's review the biblical principles from this section which you are now making part of your new mind:

1. God gave you the *power* to get wealth! (Deut. 8:18.)

2. God wants you to prosper. (3 John 2.)

3. Hard workers will have plenty of bread. (Prov. 28:19.)

4. If you do not provide for your own, you are worse than a non-believer. (1 Tim. 5:8.)

5. If you do not work, you will not eat. (2 Thess. 3:10.)

6. Jesus was a giver, and a receiver. (Luke 7:44-46.)

7. Sow much seed, and you will harvest much. (2 Cor. 9:6.)

8. Do not look at your circumstances when you

sow. (Eccl. 11:4.)

9. Sow all the time. (Eccl. 11:6.)

10. In due season, you will reap. (Gal. 6:9)

When God's spiritual laws for prosperity begin to totally transform your mind, when your life comes into absolute alignment with God's mind, then *His* abundant blessings will begin to flow into your life.

Deuteronomy 28:8 (NKJ) says: **The Lord will command the blessing on you....** Verse 2 of that same chapter says that the blessings of the Lord will "overtake" you. No matter how far from God's plan of abundance you are now, when you begin to comply with God's spiritual laws of prosperity, He will overtake you with His blessings!

Section II:
How You Can Reap in a Recession!

Lesson 8: Reaping in Recession

Recession, inflation, and economic hard times have been with mankind virtually since the beginning of time. They are not new conditions demanding new solutions. The biblical answers to these economic conditions first appear early in the book of Genesis.

> And there was a famine in the land, beside the first famine that was in the days of Abraham....
>
> **Genesis 26:1**

God gave Isaac very specific instructions to follow in order to prosper during those economic hard times:

1. Stay faithful to God's commands.

The Lord told Isaac He would bless him because ...**Abraham obeyed my voice, and kept my charge, my commandments, my statutes, and my laws** (Gen. 26:5).

Don't let circumstances ruin your good Christian habits and lifestyles. Many saints become inconsistent in times of economic pressure. Fluctuation from your Christian principles will only weaken you further.

2. Don't follow the world's philosophy.

Because of the famine, everyone was leaving to

go to Egypt, but the Lord had a different program for Isaac:

> ...**Go not down into Egypt; dwell in the land which I shall tell thee of:**
>
> **Sojourn in this land, and I will be with thee, and will bless thee....**
>
> **Genesis 26:2,3**

Move to a new city or state only upon God's command, not because of a rumor that there is prosperity there. Remember: God can bless you in *any* location.

> **Blessed shalt thou be in the city, and blessed shalt thou be in the field.**
>
> **Deuteronomy 28:3**

3. Sow generously during the famine.

Isaac went forth under the Lord's instructions, and he **...sowed in that land, and received in the same year an hundredfold: and the Lord blessed him** (Gen. 26:12).

Early on in God's precious Word He set down this principle of biblical economics. God intended for Isaac to conquer the famine, and gave him the prosperity principles to emerge victorious from it.

These same basic biblical principles apply for you and me today. Begin to use them now in your own life.

Remember:

• Stay faithful to God's commands.

• Don't follow the world's philosophy.

• Sow generously during the famine.

Lesson 9: The World's Ways Are Not God's Ways

If you want to prosper according to biblical principles, you must first forget most of the world's notions and principles of prosperity.

When everyone around Isaac was heading for Egypt, God told him to stay put — to ignore the world's answer to the famine problem — and to sow in the midst of the famine! (For complete details, see Chapter 26 of the book of Genesis.)

The world's answer was to flee.

The *Word's answer* was to stay and sow.

Ecclesiastes 11:4 clearly indicates how the world's way is different from God's way when dealing with economic matters:

> **He that observeth the wind shall not sow;**
> **and he that regardeth the clouds shall not reap.**

The people who were fleeing to Egypt in Isaac's day were looking too closely at their unpleasant circumstances. They observed the winds of hard times. They regarded the clouds of gloom and doom. So, they uprooted their families, abandoned their possessions and their homes, and headed straight for Egypt. After all, everybody was doing it. But it was sowing, not fleeing, that delivered Isaac from his circumstances. The seeds he sowed delivered him.

God told Isaac to stay and sow the seeds for a harvest in the midst of a famine. He said,

> *"Isaac, don't look at your circumstances.*
> *Don't look at the famine around you. Ignore the*
> *winds and the clouds, and focus only on your*

desired goal. Consider only your need to eat and to prosper. If you want food for your family in the midst of famine, then you must first sow the seeds that will produce the harvest."

So Isaac sowed the seeds, and God produced a harvest, without following the world's methods.

Do not listen to the world's answers, even when the winds of hard times hit your family, or the clouds of gloom and doom are all around you. Instead, seek the voice of God. His way is not the world's way.

The world says to hoard all you can in the midst of a famine. The Word of God says to plant seed, and expect to reap a harvest.

Remember:

Hard times are the wrong times to stop giving to God.

Lesson 10:
If You Want More Money

Right now you may find yourself in a situation similar to Isaac's. He was in the midst of a harsh famine, and you may be in the midst of your own harsh, economic famine.

If you live in North America, your family is probably getting enough basic foods to eat, but your "prosperity" may seem to stop right there. It may be that your paycheck just never seems to stretch far enough to pay the rent, the utilities, and to meet all your other financial obligations.

Your stomach may be full — but your pockets are empty!

So what do you do now?

Do what Isaac did:

Refuse to become fearful because of your circumstances. If you do not ignore the winds and the clouds, and do not follow God's biblical principles, you will not reap a harvest. Remember:

> **He that observeth the wind shall not sow;
> and he that regardeth the clouds shall not reap.**
> **Ecclesiastes 11:4**

In the midst of an economic famine, the world tells you to hoard your money, to watch it very closely, not to spend one dime that isn't absolutely necessary.

Yes, hard times are a time for priority-only spending; foolish waste in hard times is not godly wisdom. But, whatever you do, don't count God out of your priority giving. Remember: giving to Him is your way out of the crisis.

The world's philosophy in hard times is to hoard the little corn they have left; then they starve in the process.

Christians should always remember that some financial seeds are for eating, and some are for planting so we can have a much needed financial harvest.

If you desire more money in the midst of an economic famine, then you must begin to sow more "money seeds" that will produce for you a greater money harvest! Without the sowing of seeds, there can be no harvest. Simply stated, if you want to prosper in hard times, you must start giving more to God so He can release more finances to you.

Whatever you do, don't feel that you are the

only one with financial problems. Everyone goes through hard economic situations from time to time. But don't make the fatal mistake of "tightening up" with God when things get "tight!"

Remember Isaac. He was one of God's children, and he obeyed God's laws. He planted good, valuable seed in a time when everyone else was hoarding seeds — and his seed came up, even in the midst of a famine! Why? Because he planted in accordance with God's command.

If you want more money in your hands each month, then plant more "money seeds" into the Gospel each month. When a child of God plants money seeds, he has God's Word that a money harvest will come up, even in the midst of the worst economic famine.

Lesson 11: Give Away What You Lack

In the last few lessons, you have learned how God wants us to deal with famine. You saw how Isaac survived the famine through his obedience to God and his willingness to plant precious seed in the midst of famine. When you find yourself in the midst of an economic famine, it is important that you remember this important warning:

Do not eat too much of the seed corn.

Some should be eaten, but some must be planted!

Look at how God rewarded the widow at Zarephath for her willingness to obey God and follow His principles of biblical economics. (You will find the complete details of this story in 1 Kings 17:8-16.)

This poor widow was nearly out of food. She had only enough for one final meal. When the prophet Elijah came and asked her for "a morsel of bread," she replied:

> ...I have not a cake, but (only) an handful of meal in a barrel,...and, behold, I am gathering two sticks, that I may go in and dress (prepare) it for me and my son, that we may eat it, and die.
>
> 1 Kings 17:12

This woman was experiencing her own personal famine. She was down to her last meal! But Elijah exhorted her to share her last cake with him. (In this situation, the prophet Elijah represented God, much in the same way that churches and ministries do today.) He promised her that if she obeyed, then:

> ...The barrel of meal shall not waste (be used up),...until the day that the Lord sendeth rain upon the earth.
>
> 1 Kings 17:14

The turning point was when the woman actually gave the last of her precious food away. The world would have told her that it was sensible to hoard her small bit of remaining meal, to keep what little she had for herself and her son before they died.

But, God works by different principles. This lady was exhorted to share her meal with God's minister, and then let God provide the harvest. She planted seed in the darkest part of the famine, because Elijah convinced her that if she planted, she would reap a bountiful harvest.

So the poor widow obeyed, and met the need of the man of God. As a result of her willingness to plant seeds, and her refusal to observe the winds and clouds of famine, God miraculously met her need.

> **...the barrel of meal wasted not (was not used up),....according to the word of the Lord, which he spake by Elijah.**
>
> **1 Kings 17:16**

Remember: the golden rule works with God as well as with man. What you want done for you, you must first do for others. When you help meet the needs of God and His workers, He will meet your needs.

> **Whatever you want men to do to you, do also to them....**
>
> **Matthew 7:12 NKJ**

Lesson 12: Plant in Good Ground

Simply sowing seed is not enough to produce a harvest; you must be very careful where you sow. If you throw all your seed onto a concrete slab, you will not reap a harvest.

One key principle of biblical economics is that you must always sow your seeds in good ground.

Remember: the best and most fertile ground in which you can plant your seed is the ground consecrated and dedicated to producing a harvest for the sons and daughters of God. Don't let sentimentalism or sectarian allegiance sway you away from the best ground in which to plant your seed.

When times are financially difficult, you can reap your most abundant harvest by planting your precious seeds into God's proven, producing works.

Your economic circumstances determine the value of the seeds you plant!

The money seeds of God's children are the most precious when they are scarce. When the money seeds you want to put into God's work are very scarce, take comfort and let your faith grow by what God says about your precious seed:

> He that goeth forth and weepeth, *bearing precious seed,* shall doubtless come again with rejoicing, bringing his sheaves with him.
>
> **Psalm 126:6**

Now, that verse should give you comfort and boldness to give to God's work even in tight financial times. God absolutely guarantees that precious seed will produce a return; His Word says that he who sows it "shall doubtless come again with rejoicing."

Your precious seed has a guarantee of success and harvest!

God's Word abounds with *biblical keys* that will open the very treasure house of God for you. One of these keys, and perhaps the most vital of all, is the knowledge that you must plant your seeds in good fertile ground if you are to reap the best harvest. Very carefully pick the ministries you invest in — those Christ-honoring, soul-winning, Word-centered ministries which properly manage the money they are given.

Don't forget: when the dark clouds of hard times come into your life, God's Word can guide you out of your difficulty and into good times. Always remember that following God's direction in your giving won't lead you into trouble, but it will lead you out of it. God knows how much you give and how much of the precious seed you have left. So, when your finances get "tight," don't stop giving! Plant your precious seeds very carefully in good ground, and God will return an abundant harvest to you.

Lesson 13:
Nothing Is "Luck" with God

The principles God established in His Word to guide you are absolute. They are not subject to luck. The widow at Zarephath gave from her scarce food supply, and she received her food supply back from God, multiplied.

This return was not luck — it was the result of a direct application of God's Law of Increase. The widow *gave* from her precious meal, and God *returned* an abundance of precious meal to her, in fulfillment of the divine principle found in His Word:

> **Give, and it shall be given unto you....For with the same measure that ye mete withal (measure) it shall be measured to you again.**
>
> **Luke 6:38**

I cannot emphasize this truth enough. The widow did not run into a streak of good luck. She obeyed God, and gave from her precious seed. God *honored His Word* by bestowing His abundant blessings upon her! God, seeing her meager resources, realized that she had given generously. He knew that this woman's gift to His servant was a great sacrificial measure — it was her last cake, all that stood between her and starvation. God's Word says that she received in return a very large measure from God — an unending supply of meal and oil!

Luke tells of another poor widow who gave out of her poverty and need. Seeing her cast two small coins into the temple treasury, Jesus said that she had given more than any of the others:

> **For all these have of their abundance cast in
> unto the offerings of God: but she of her penury
> (poverty or need) hath cast in all the living that she
> had.**
>
> Luke 21:4

Jesus not only saw into her pocketbook, He saw into her heart! Her "measure" was without a doubt greater than that of any rich man in the temple. She gave "all the living that she had" with a heart of expectation and love.

Are you starting to grasp the spiritual principles in these examples? The two widows did not run into a streak of luck; they actually set in motion a principle of biblical economics. They loosed the superior spiritual principles of God to work in the midst of their circumstances. They literally left the realm of chance and committed their future well-being to God's promises instead of depending on the whims of economic circumstances.

Maybe right now you are like these widows. Your money supply is scarce, and your gift to the Gospel will come only from "precious seed." You have a choice. You can hoard your seed, or you can do as these widows did, and give out of your scarcity.

When you give, know that you are not subject to the whimsical fate of luck; instead, you are anchoring your future to God's superior principles of biblical economics. The heavenly Father will honor your faith. Scripture shows that when we measure out our best to God, He measures out His best to us.

Leave the realm of fate and enter the realm of faith.

Lesson 14: How to Start Reaping Now!

If you want to start reaping financial blessings in your life right now, you must follow the principles God has given in Scripture.

Isaac sowed his seed in famine, when everyone around him was hoarding their seed and fleeing to Egypt.

The widow at Zarephath fed the man of God from her last bit of meal; she provided him with a cake scraped up from the "bottom of the barrel."

The poor widow at the temple gave "all of the living she had" in the offering.

In all three cases, these desperate people *began to reap* by following three basic principles:

1. They started right where they were at the point of their need.

2. They planted precious seeds, despite their circumstances. Each refused to observe the winds and clouds of gloom and doom.

3. They planted out of their lack, their need. They gave their precious seeds in extremely hard times, and all three received God's abundant blessing in their lives in the midst of hard times.

The same spiritual principles which allowed Isaac and the two widows to start reaping, will work for you too!

If you want to begin reaping God's blessings,

then start sowing your precious seed into the Gospel, and it will return to you, multiplied!

> **They that sow in tears** (hard times) **shall reap in joy.**

> **He that goeth forth and weepeth, bearing precious seed** (the last seed from the "bottom of the barrel"), **shall doubtless come again with rejoicing, bringing his sheaves with him.**

> **Psalm 126:5,6**

Notice God's promise to you: sow precious seed into the Kingdom of God and you *shall doubtless* rejoice when you receive the harvest from your seed-sowing.

This is not a matter of luck. This is not a matter of hard work (although God honors hard work too).

This is a matter of obedience. When you are obedient to God's Word, God will honor His Word and will fulfill His promises.

It is a matter of law, God's Law — laws we must always obey, and which God will not deny.

How You Can Reap in Recession In Summary

You should be experiencing the biblical process of mind transformation as you study these lessons. Remember, I told you God's way to change your mind is precept upon precept, line upon line, here a little, there a little.

With each new lesson and precept, your mind is filtering out the mistaken ideas that are polluting the precious living waters of God's Word in your mind. With each new biblical concept you accept from God's Word, you are displacing an old, destructive concept from your mind; you are becoming closer and closer to what God would have you become!

For years, the devil has told you that most people are prosperous because they are lucky. Hopefully, that old worldly concept is now being rooted out of your mind, and is being replaced with God's sound biblical concepts:

When you sow precious seed, you will doubtless reap a harvest. It has nothing at all to do with luck — it is according to a principle of biblical economics.

For years the devil has told you that when you experience tight financial times, you must hold onto every penny you have and slow down your giving to God.

Hopefully that old erroneous concept is now gone from your mind, and you have replaced it with the biblical principle which guarantees us that we will receive a harvest — rejoicing — when we plant our precious seed!

Isaac sowed in hard times, and reaped in good measure!

The two widows sowed in hard times, and reaped in good measure!

And now, if you, too, will sow in hard times, surely you will reap in good measure!

Participate in this proven process!

Continue to read one lesson in the morning, and reread it again in the evening. Allow the new thoughts and ideas from each page to transform your mind.

Remember, Satan wants you in financial bondage — in a constant unbroken cycle of lack. He knows that as long as you are always struggling to pay the bills, you cannot give the much-needed funds you desire to give to God's great end-time harvest.

Satan also knows that when you begin to *grasp and apply* these biblical principles in your life, you will begin to receive the abundance you need in order to give to every good ministry God lays on your heart.

Yes, even Satan knows that if you apply these biblical principles, you will reap a mighty blessing, and will want to be a good steward of the riches God *will doubtless* bring into your life.

Do not be deceived. These new concepts — these new biblical principles — are of absolutely no value to you until you step out in faith and begin to apply them in your daily living. Nothing will happen until you put these principles into practice.

So begin today.

Give. Give what you need, remembering that **...whatsoever a man soweth, that shall he also reap** (Gal. 6:7).

Give to the Gospel.

Plant your precious seeds in fertile ground, and watch God unfold a financial miracle in your life!

Section III
God — the Greatest Giver!

Lesson 15: God Freely Gives All Things

God has always been a great giver!

> For by grace are ye saved through faith; and that not of yourselves: *it is the gift of God:*
>
> Not of works, lest any man should boast.
>
> **Ephesians 2:8,9**

You see, it is God's nature to give. *God the Father freely gives us all things!* Our very salvation is a free gift from God.

> He that spared not his own Son, but delivered him up for us all, how shall he not with him also *freely give us all things?*
>
> **Romans 8:32**

Notice that God wants to give us "all things" — not just those things that are spiritual, or heavenly, but all things! That includes money for food, clothing, rent, gas, and even something left over for entertainment.

All things.

If we realize that God did not withhold His own Son (nothing was more precious than His own Son, Jesus), then it is not difficult to understand that God will give us all things. If we can focus on the greatest Gift, Jesus Christ — and the fact that this gift has already been given to us — then no lands, houses, treasures, or any other good thing we need will be withheld from us.

Even the Holy Ghost is freely given to all who ask for Him:

> If ye then, being evil, know how to give good gifts unto your children: how much more shall your heavenly Father *give the Holy Spirit to them that ask him?*
>
> Luke 11:13

Let this concept sink into your spirit. Our God is a giving God! He desires to give us *all things*:

> According as his divine power hath given unto us *all things* that pertain unto life and godliness....
>
> 2 Peter 1:3

God is the Supreme Giver of the universe. He gives to us according to His divine power! He desires that we have all things that pertain to life and godliness. Get that truth into your spirit and force out any thoughts that do not come into conformity with this promise from God!

Lesson 16: God Wants You To Be Like Him!

Man is created in the image of God, but Satan changed that image when mankind fell into sin. But those who accept Jesus Christ are restored and brought into the image of God once again. Yes, God wants you to be like Him! He literally envisions you like Himself:

> ...as he (Jesus) is, so are we in this world.
>
> 1 John 4:17

You know that God is a giver.

You know that Jesus is a giver.

And, you know that the Holy Spirit is a giver.

Now, it is important for you to understand that God wants *you* to be a giver! Jesus constantly urged His disciples to give:

1. He told them to give to all who ask. (Luke 6:30.)

2. He told them that freely they had received, and freely they should give. (Matt. 10:8.)

3. He urged them to give the people food to eat. (Luke 9:13.)

4. He taught, "Give, and it shall be given unto you." (Luke 6:38.)

5. He urged us to give to the poor. (Mark 14:7.)

Jesus lived a lifestyle of giving. He said:

> **...I am come that they might have life, and that they might have it more abundantly.**
>
> **John 10:10**

Yes, God wants you and me to be like His Son, Jesus — not just in a future life when we will be like Him, but right now, by imitating Him.

You can start by taking hold of His wonderful characteristic of giving. Begin to see yourself as a great giver too. The giving of Jesus Christ went into every realm. When He met the depressed, He *gave* them a light heart; when He came across the hungry, He *gave* them food to eat; when He encountered the naked, He *gave* them clothes to wear.

Jesus *gave* and *gave* and *gave* and *gave*.

Finally, He made the ultimate sacrifice — He *gave* His life, so we could have eternal life!

You may never be called upon to give your life's blood for another person; but, starting today, you can literally become a giver of every good thing needed by those around you.

Remember that with each act of giving, you will receive; so that one day, if you continue in faithful giving, you will have enough to give in every way God desires.

Remember: you are becoming like God — not all at once, but step by step, progressively, from glory to glory.

Lesson 17:
Give Joyfully, Reap Abundantly

God freely gives His gifts to us. Our salvation comes to us freely. The Holy Spirit is given freely. And the gifts of the Spirit are given freely.

God expects from us the same willingness to give freely:

> ...so let him give; not grudgingly, or of necessity: for *God loveth a cheerful giver.*
>> **2 Corinthians 9:7**

The next time you write out a check to your local church or favorite ministry, remember that the Lord desires you to give with a "cheerful" heart. Sing a sacred song as you write out that check. Think of the joy your money will bring to the lives of those who will be saved or delivered through it. Put a big smile on your face when you drop your next offering into the collection basket.

As you give with your cheerful heart, remember that you must also give abundantly if you want to reap abundantly:

> **But this I say, He which soweth sparingly shall reap also sparingly; and he which soweth bountifully shall reap also bountifully.**
>
> **2 Corinthians 9:6**

At first, this scripture may seem a bit unfair. You could easily be thinking: "But, Brother John, I don't have a lot to give. I have only a small amount of money each week that I can give to God's work. I guess that means that I will reap sparingly.

That is not true! Remember the poor widow with the two mites? Jesus said she gave *more* than all the rich men in the temple. Why? Because by her giving, in proportion to her income, she made a much greater sacrifice than anyone else! Jesus saw her heart. The poor widow gave "bountifully," and God rewarded her bountifully. Remember: "with the same measure" you give, God will give back to you again.

When you give "bountifully" from your own supply of money, keep in mind that it is the *proportion* of the whole amount that you give — not the amount itself — which determines whether your gift is bountiful. Give with a "cheerful heart" and God will abundantly bless you.

So do not be discouraged if your offerings to God are not as much as you would like them to be.

God looks at your offerings in relation to how much you have left after you give.

Lesson 18: Giving Always Results in Receiving

Memorize the title of today's study. It is a vital principle of biblical economics:

Giving Always Results in Receiving!

No exceptions. You have God's Word on it:

> **Give, and it shall be given unto you;** *good measure, pressed down,* **and** *shaken together,* **and** *running over,* **shall men give into your bosom. For with the same measure that ye mete withal (measure) it shall be measured to you** *again.*
>
> **Luke 6:38**

Look closely at these *key points:*

1. God promises to return your gift to you. He says *you will receive* a "good measure," literally "running over." God will abundantly bless you when you give to Him.

2. God says that your blessings will come from "men" who shall give "into your bosom." God uses people, and so He has no difficulty blessing you from *unexpected* places. The source God uses isn't important; what is vital is that you understand the biblical principle — when you give, you will receive a return.

3. By the same measure you give, you will receive. Remember: the "measure" is not *how much* you give, but how much you give *in proportion to your income.* This scripture does not promise that if you give five dollars, you will receive five dollars in

return. It says that if you give five dollars and that sum is simply casual pocket money, then you will not receive a very big "measure" in return. You will receive the five dollars back, but not in a greatly multiplied measure.

But, if that five dollars is a very critical part of your remaining funds, a precious seed out of your limited remaining resources — then it becomes a "great measure" in God's eyes, and you will receive a "great measure" in return from Him; your gift will be greatly multiplied.

When you become a giver, you automatically move yourself into the realm of a receiver. There are no exceptions to this rule. However, there are levels of receiving: **...some thirty, and some sixty, and some an hundred**(fold) (Mark 4:8). The measure you use in giving will determine the measure that will be applied to you in receiving. No matter with what measure your gift is made, when you give to God, you *will* receive a return on your giving: **Give, and it shall be given unto you**...(Luke 6:38).

Remember:

> **Be not deceived** (don't be fooled); **God is not mocked** (He cannot be fooled): **for whatsoever a man soweth, that shall he also reap.**
>
> **Galatians 6:7**

Now you understand why the title of this lesson is so important. Do not forget it! Giving always results in receiving.

Lesson 19:
Giving Is Your God-Given Right

Look again at Luke 6:38:

> **Give, and it shall be given unto you; good measure, pressed down, and shaken together, and running over, shall men give into your bosom. For with the same measure that ye mete withal (measure) it shall be measured to you again.**

These promises are not restricted to any particular group of saints; it is every saint's right to claim them, if he or she puts into action God's principle of giving.

Day by day your mind is being transformed, precept upon precept, line upon line, until you come to fully understand what a joy and a God-given right it is for you to be a giver.

Imagine that your local bank promised you that every time you wrote a check, it would credit your account with "more than enough" funds to cover the draft. Surely you would consider yourself a very fortunate person. At first, you would probably be a bit cautious, and write checks for moderate amounts. But, as the bank proved itself faithful and honored your checks again and again, putting more and more money into your account, you would soon realize that this wonderful new relationship was opening up a whole new life to you and your loved ones. Not only would it be a blessing to you, but any neighbor or friend who found out about your bank would want the "right" to the same sort of account. It would be wrong for your bank to offer this program to you alone.

Of course, we know that banks don't operate this way; but God clearly declares that He does!

He promises to give us back more than we give, and He guarantees this return to all His "depositors" (all those who give to His work). When I say "all," I mean *all!* God declares in His Word that He is no respecter of persons. More than once He promises that we will receive in return *more than we give* — every single time!

Are you grasping that truth?

Since the entire resources of the universe are at His creative disposal, our heavenly Father will never run out of funds. He will always be able to meet His promise of giving back to us more than we give to Him.

Do you see what this message is doing to your thinking about giving to God? Giving to Him is not an obligation — it is an *opportunity* to put God's biblical principles into action! It is a chance to begin operating your heavenly checking account according to a principle that contradicts the world: *the more you give away to God's work, the more He will return to you so you can give to His work again!*

> **Yes, God will give you much so that you can give away much....**
> **2 Corinthians 9:11 tlb**

If the entire Body of Christ began to operate in accordance with this biblical principle, we would witness the abundance Moses experienced in the book of Exodus. His people were so willing to give to build the sanctuary that Moses finally had to stop the giving.

> ...Let neither man nor woman make any more work for the offering of the sanctuary. So the people were restrained from bringing.
>
> For the stuff they had was sufficient for all the work to make it, and *too much*.
>
> **Exodus 36:6,7**

Begin to grasp your God-given right of giving. Act upon God's promise to return to you more than you give. If you will do so, there will come a day when the abundance of God will literally overtake you. You will have enough money to fulfill every desire to give to God, with plenty left over to meet your every need and desire.

Lesson 20: God's Will for You — More Than Enough

When you give to God, your gift allows God the opportunity to bless you, to keep His promises, and to give you more than enough. By your faithful obedience in giving your tithes and offerings, you set into motion God's biblical principles of economics. Your precious gifts unleash God's power in several areas of your life.

1. Your gift will prosper you. God promises that when you are a giver, your gift will increase and multiply:

> A gift...whithersoever it turneth, it prospereth.
>
> **Proverbs 17:8**

2. Your gift will provide you a place in life, and will bring you before "great" (godly) men in society:

> **A man's gift maketh room for him, and bringeth him before great men.**
>
> **Proverbs 18:16**

3. Your gift will even bring you friends:

> **...every man is a friend to him that giveth gifts.**
>
> **Proverbs 19:6**

This does not advocate buying friends with your money. It simply means that your giving sets up a magnetism that draws others to you.

4. Your gift will stop anger that is focused against you:

> **A gift in secret pacifieth anger....**
>
> **Proverbs 21:14**

Just for fun, try this when someone is angry with you. Send that person a secret gift and watch his anger quiet down. Don't ask me how it works; I don't know. But it does work, for I have seen it do so again and again.

Do you understand what God intends to do to your life when you give?

When you are a cheerful giver, God will bless you and give you back many blessings — out of His abundance!

God cares about *you*, and He ministers to you in many areas when you unleash the biblical process of giving. Not only does He minister to you in the area of finances, He also ministers to you spiritually, and to those around you. Being a great giver produces a positive, cooperative atmosphere all around you!

Lesson 21:
Giving Will Spread the Gospel

In lesson 19, you read how Moses was overwhelmed by the generosity of the Israelites and asked them to stop giving. They had literally given too much!

I believe that if enough Christians grasp the principles of biblical economics in this book and then apply them in their daily lives, every church, every mission outreach, every Christian television ministry — and yes, every Christian home in our world — will scream, "Stop, Lord, we've got *too much!*"

Your faithfulness in giving to God's work guarantees that a day of abundant prosperity will eventually come to you, a time when the reapers will overtake the sowers. But no matter how long it takes the whole church world to come to that moment, you can begin right now to have more than enough by applying these principles and seeing their benefits materialize in your life before your very eyes.

That is not *my* promise; it is *God's* promise!

When you learn to act upon this promise, you can, without fear, ask God how large your special financial gift should be to a certain Christian television ministry, a strong missionary outreach, or to your own local church. Whatever God tells you to do, you will have the money to do it — when you catch this God-given vision!

Remember, giving is a *key* part of your Christian walk. It is not a separate, non-spiritual act of writing out a check. Giving of your finances to God is a deep, personal interaction with God Himself, and is as much a part of your Christianity as your time of prayer.

So do not just give your money without thought or without prayer. Ask God where you should direct your gifts, and even ask Him how much you should give. God has a definite plan for your finances, and He cares about your individual offerings.

Nearly 20 percent of all the verses in the Bible relate to finances, land, money, goods, cattle, personal belongings, and so on — in various forms — so you can be sure God is concerned about your personal possessions and finances.

He cares about every part of your life, and each part relates to your overall walk as a Christian.

Remember: God is a great giver, and He wants you to be one too:

> How then shall they call on him in whom they have not believed? and how shall they believe in him of whom they have not heard? and how shall they hear without a preacher?
>
> And how shall they preach, except they be sent?....
>
> Romans 10:14,15

I believe there is an answer to this crucial question. They will be sent by those who put God's plan of giving and receiving to work until they have complete dominion over every aspect of their finances!

God — The Greatest Giver In Summary

Giving started with God. He set the example, He demonstrated how to give, and He has determined the rewards of giving.

If you are uncomfortable with any of the concepts you have learned in the past few lessons, don't argue with me. These are not Brother John's ideas; they are God's!

Brother John did not decide that you should give away what you lack — *God did*.

Brother John did not decide that what you sow, you will reap — *God did*.

Brother John did not decide to declare to you, "If you give, you will receive an abundant return on your investment" — *that's God's idea*.

If this message bothers you, talk to God about it — it's His idea, not mine!

Why are some of us so set in our old ways of thinking that we simply label anything as "untrue" if it does not agree with our preconceived concepts?

Truth aligns with God's concepts, not with our own ideas. Whether we agree or not, God will prosper those who give to His work! God will bless those who give, and He will bless them in proportion to the "measure" that they give. Those who give sacrificially will receive a greater return from God than those who give out of their abundance. You see, God knows the difference in discretionary funds and non-discretionary funds; He cannot be fooled.

Remember: that's not my idea — it's God's!

All I am doing is reporting to you in context the verses of Scripture many preachers ignore because of the controversy and turmoil they produce among the carnal-minded "saints"!

The verses that talk about God's desire for you to prosper and be successful did not come from a recent, revised edition of the Bible! They were not just uncovered in the Dead Sea scrolls. The verses you are reading have been in the Bible since it was first inspired by the Holy Ghost to the sacred writers.

Because the verses pertaining to the finances of the saints have not been properly applied over the past 2,000 years, the Church of God is now weak, anemic, under-financed, and must beg each week for the funds to keep going; then it must spend those hard-earned tithes and offerings on mortgage payments while the world cries for spiritual ministry.

That's not what God intended.

Here is the challenge. If you will apply God's principles of Biblical economics in your own life, if you will muster the courage to unleash the process by giving, then your finances will be blessed abundantly, and God's Church will begin to grow beyond anything we can imagine.

Ministers will be trained and sent forth, because there will be "more than enough" money to send them.

Television programs will beam the Gospel around the world, because there will be "more than enough" money to buy the air time.

Churches will expand to hold the ever-increasing numbers of people attracted by the "new" Christians who always have "more than enough," even in the midst of "famine"!

This is exactly what John had in mind when he expressed his wonderful wish for each of us in 3 John 2:

> **Beloved, I wish above all things that thou mayest prosper and be in health, even as thy soul prospereth.**

You have two choices: 1) You can hold onto your old, traditional beliefs and continue to struggle from paycheck to paycheck. 2) You can *apply* God's economic principles in your own life, and cheerfully give in "good measure."

If every person who reads this book will choose the second option, and begin to freely and joyfully give of his or her finances in *"good measure,"* soon preachers and ministries all over the world will be screaming:

"Stop! Stop! We have enough! The end-time harvest is now assured."

And, God's people — His children — overwhelmed by God's love, will shout:

"Heavenly Father, You have given us a blessing so large we cannot contain it! Truly it is as the Scriptures say: There is more than enough"!

Section IV:
Ten Truths About Money

Lesson 22: Finances Are Important!

If something is important to God, *and* it has a very high priority on God's list of worthwhile subjects, don't you think it should be important to you?

By now, I pray it is firmly rooted into your spirit that *God does desire good things for you.* Not only does He want you to be spiritually strong and prosperous, He also desires you to be prosperous in the material areas of your life and your family. He wants you to have food, clothing, housing, finances — and yes, even everything that pertains to the "good life."

God did not tell Isaac to forget about the famine and be spiritual. Instead, He told him: first, where to live; second, what to plant; and third, what to expect from his sowing. God wanted Isaac to have the material things necessary to live well, even in the midst of famine!

You see, God *does* care about your material needs.

The Old and New Testament talk so much about "seeds" and "planting" because at the time they were written, the world was operating in an agricultural economy. Jesus simply related to the agricultural times in which He lived. If Jesus were walking on the earth today, He would have a significant amount to say about home mortgages, trust deeds, government bonds, interest rates, mass production, and marketing trends. All of these topics would be liberally dispensed among the parables and similes He would recount.

Today it seems it is just fine for preachers to talk about religious matters, but somehow it is felt that the topic of money and practical things is not spiritual and should not be discussed by God's men.

Nonsense! Money is to be a spiritual issue to the saints of God!

When the poor widow sacrificed her two mites in an offering in the temple, Jesus did not say: "Woman, your financial sacrifice does not matter to me. God is not interested in your money. All that matters to God is your spiritual needs. I'm not concerned about your material needs. Just learn to grin and bear your financial condition."

Instead, Jesus praised her for her precious financial sacrifice. Jesus knew the widow's heart! Since the mites were a big part of her necessary living expenses, Jesus considered them a significant gift. Her giving was an important action! Her gift was comparable to the gifts given by others that day, including those given by very rich people. Jesus even called over the disciples and made open comment about the faith of the widow as it was manifested in her money offering.

You see, money is *important* to God. Money is important to Jesus. So, money should be important to you. In the next few weeks, let your mind and spirit grow into a deeper understanding of the *value* of money — to you, to God and to the spreading of the Gospel.

Lesson 23:
Money Is Not Evil

One of the biggest mistakes about money comes from a misunderstanding of 1 Timothy 6:10:

> For *the love of* money is the root of all evil....

The mistake made here by the saints of God is in what they think the verse says. Read it carefully: "For the love of money is the root of all evil."

Now, many people do not read what the Bible really says. Instead, they read what *they want the Bible to say*. Please notice that this verse does not say that money is evil! It clearly states that the *love* of money is the root of all evil. Nothing at all is said about money itself in verse 10; all it says is that *the love of money* is at the root of all evil.

Yet, I've heard so many good Christians use this verse to justify their belief that God does not want them to have anything to do with money. They ignorantly believe that the Bible teaches that money is evil.

This is a terrible mistake. God *does* want you to have money. God *does* care about your needs, and He knows that the lack of money can cause very serious problems in your life, as well as throughout society. It doesn't take a genius to notice that people are holding up gas stations because they do not have money. All over the world, people are starving to death because they do not have money to buy food. People are freezing because they do not have enough money to buy fuel to heat their homes. People with poor health could be well if they had the money to buy proper food.

The Bible even says, **...money answereth all things** (Eccl. 10:19). Money itself is neither good nor evil. It only has the ability to do what its owner wants it to do. The owner is in charge. The money is neither good nor bad; it is whatever its owner is. It serves him *without question;* it is ready to do good or evil at its owner's discretion.

My money is good money. The only way for money to do anything evil is for it to come under the control of an evil person. The Bible tells me that if I believe in the Lord Jesus Christ, and live after the precepts He has taught me, then I am a good man. And when I spend my money, I spend it for good things.

My money is spent on spreading the Gospel of Jesus Christ, on my family and their needs, and on helping others less fortunate than I.

My money is not evil. The only way for money to be "evil" is for it to come under the control of an evil person. Money simply manifests what is in its owner's heart. When the poor widow gave her two mites, she showed Jesus she cared enough to give out of her want. Because she was a good woman, her money was "good money," and rather than loving it, she quickly and totally gave it into the offering in God's temple.

Luke 12:34 says, **For where your treasure is, there will your heart be also.**

If your heart is in line with God, then your treasure (your money) will literally be godly money.

When your heart is right, you will put more and more of your money into the Gospel and less and less money into recreation and frivolous diversions.

Mark this truth: *money is not evil.* It is a magnificent tool in the hands of godly men and women to help bring the saving message of Jesus Christ to lost souls around the world! Stretch your faith to see that God wants you to have as much money as you will use properly.

Remember:

> ...God will give you much so that you can give away much....
>
> 2 Corinthians 9:11 TLB

Lesson 24: Improper Attitudes Toward Money Can Harm You

When talking about money, as in discussing any other topic in Scripture, it is important to maintain a balance. In the last lesson we determined that money is not evil. In this lesson, I would like to plant in your thinking the proper balance on this controversial topic. Money can harm you, because it is very powerful.

Money *does* have the potential to harm you if you do not control it in accordance with God's specific instructions. It can harm you, for example, if you use it for dark and sinful purposes. It can harm you if you use it to buy destructive substances (drugs or narcotics). It can hurt you and others if you use it to fulfill the lusts of the flesh instead of the will of the Spirit.

In Matthew 19 Jesus told the rich young ruler to sell all he had and to follow Him. When the young ruler could not give up his wealth, he proved that he was not in control of his riches. Instead, his riches controlled him! Don't think for a moment that his money did not hurt him. It literally cost him his soul!

Money does have the potential to harm you if you cannot control it in accordance with God's will for your life! You are in real danger of your money hurting you whenever it begins to rule you, instead of *your ruling it*.

The "love of money" caused Judas Iscariot to betray Jesus. For just thirty pieces of silver, he handed Jesus over to be crucified, and lost his own soul.

When used improperly, or when given improper importance, money can *definitely* cause harm. Begin to view money as any other tool you have available for your use. How you use that tool will determine whether it does harm or good.

Gasoline. Electricity. Guns. Cars. Explosives. Nuclear power. Airplanes. Money. All of these things can improve the quality of man's life. And, all can cause severe harm when misused or out of control. Their blessing or harm to your life is determined by whether they are operated under your control or are out of control.

Money can do many good things, but when money is not controlled by the Spirit of God in us, it can literally destroy us.

So don't be so naive as to think that money won't hurt you. It is very capable, if misused, of doing eternal damage.

Lesson 25: Money Doesn't Guarantee Happiness

Many of the things which make us unhappy can be "cured" by money. For example, a father who is unhappy because he does not have the money to provide food for his family will be happy when his paycheck comes.

But, money itself *never* guarantees happiness.

Think about this statement. If money guaranteed happiness, then all the rich folks would be marvelously happy, and all the poor folks would be miserably sad. You and I know that this is not the case. Rich people commit suicide. Rich people visit psychologists to treat their depression. Rich people deal with "unhappy" issues such as divorce, alcoholism, drug addiction — and yes, even financial problems. Many rich people spend the early part of their lives in misery, trying to accumulate their fortune, and then spend the latter part of their lives in misery trying to hold on to the fortune they have accumulated.

Money simply does not guarantee happiness. True happiness and lasting peace will only come through a proper relationship with Jesus:

> For the kingdom of God *is not food and drink,* but righteousness and peace and joy *in* the Holy Spirit.
>
> For he who serves Christ in these things is acceptable to God and approved by men.
>
> Therefore let us pursue the things which make for peace and the things by which one may edify another.
>
> **Romans 14:17-19** NKJ

When your relationship with God is right, your money will not cause you problems and unhappiness: instead, it will be a blessing and a source of happiness for you and others around you.

The blessing of the Lord, it maketh rich,
and *he addeth no sorrow with it.*

Proverbs 10:22

God will not harm you by multiplying money back to you. When you have the right heart and the right spirit in giving your money to Him, God will grant you riches. Although your God-given wealth will not guarantee you happiness, God does promise that the riches He gives you will not bring you sorrow. You see, righteousness, peace, and joy are found in God, not in money.

Lesson 26: People Are Not "Destined" to Be Poor

Have you ever said to yourself, "I guess I'm just not meant to be rich. I must be destined to be poor, so I suppose it's time I accept my lot in life."

Many of the saints believe this way. They believe God has somehow ordained a select few people to have all the wealth, and the rest to struggle in poverty all of their lives.

Notice the satanic deception in this statement. If you accept this lie, it immediately releases you from any responsibility for your financial circumstances and places the blame for your insufficiency on God.

For God to determine that certain select individuals are to be rich, and other people are to be poor, is unfair. It is against God's divine nature and His stated Word.

Instead, God has given to all of us *strict spiritual laws* which determine who remains poor and who becomes prosperous. These laws for poverty and prosperity are clearly stated in God's Word and are as absolute as the spiritual laws which govern salvation.

The *Law of Poverty* says: If you are lazy and do not work, you will not receive provision. (See Prov. 24:33,34.)

The *Law of Prosperity* says: If you are not lazy, if you will work without constant supervision, if you are liberal in your giving and put Jesus first in your finances, then you will be prosperous. (See Prov. 6:6-8 and Prov. 11:24,25.)

God has given us these and other guidelines throughout Scripture as His *strict spiritual laws*. When they are applied, they will determine the measure of prosperity or poverty you will experience in your own life.

If you are interested in winning the world to Christ, then it is important for you to understand these spiritual laws of prosperity.

• Operating churches costs money.

• Printing Bibles costs money.

• Preaching the Word in foreign lands costs money.

• Beaming godly television programs around the world costs money.

• Money will come to the saints when they begin to understand *and* apply God's laws of abundance in their lives.

God says that the good life is each saint's portion:

> **It is good and fitting for one to eat and drink, and to enjoy the good of all his labor...for it is his** (portion)
>
> **....Every man to whom God has given riches and wealth, and given him power to eat of it, to receive his** (portion) **and rejoice in his labor — this is the gift of God.**
>
> Ecclesiastes 5:18,19 NKJ

After reading this scripture, it is impossible to believe that only a few are destined to wealth and the rest are destined to poverty. God has made His plan very clear in His Word!

Lesson 27: God Wants You To Be Prosperous

Many Christians honestly believe that poverty is godly. They think that if a Christian is poor, he must really be in the center of God's will. There are even misguided groups of people who believe that by taking "vows of poverty," they will somehow be more godly or more believable to those who hear them witness the Gospel. Many preachers have actually taught that if we have holes in our britches and no soles on our shoes, we are suffering for Jesus and making our testimony easier to believe!

It is time for the saints to start believing God's Word instead of their own ideas!

God's Word does not teach poverty!

I am going to share with you a scripture that is so mind-shattering that I recommend you read the entire passage several times and let the truth of this shocking biblical concept begin to penetrate your spirit. It is without a doubt one of the greatest blows to the erroneous teaching that poverty enhances the testimony of the Gospel. (There is space here for only the final line. See your Bible for the entire text.)

> **Then said I, Wisdom is better than strength: nevertheless *the poor man's wisdom is despised, and his words are not heard.***
>
> **Ecclesiastes 9:16**

Don't let your traditional thinking close your mind and prevent you from seeing the real truth here: *God wants you to prosper.*

If you do not prosper, *the world will not listen to your "wisdom"* when you share the Gospel. Sure, a few will listen to your testimony even if you are poor, but many, many more will listen to your testimony if you are prosperous!

We're talking about a miracle realm.

God wants to work a miracle beyond the miracle of salvation, beyond the miracle of the Holy Ghost, and even beyond the miracle of divine health. God wants to work a miracle of financial prosperity in your life. He wants to set you up as one of His earthly stewards.

Remember 3 John 2:

> **Beloved, I wish above all things that thou mayest prosper and be in health, even as thy soul prospereth.**

When an opportunity arises for you to give, then give. Even go beyond that opportunity to look for new ones. Be bold. Ask your pastor, or your favorite television ministry, or your trusted ministry partner what they need.

When you get hold of the truth of God's will for your prosperity, you will experience such abundance you will need to find new opportunities to give. Begin to see in your spirit a whole new kind of relationship between the leaders of churches, ministries and television outreaches. Begin now to seed into God's work so He can begin to unleash His miracle of financial prosperity in your life. As God blesses you, your testimony will be a powerful witness for Him. And, as people see that there is positive financial activity around you, they will seek your opinions, and give you the opportunity to freely and effectively witness to them about your God and His Son, Jesus Christ.

Lesson 28: You Can Increase Your Finances

By now, I hope you are beginning to understand that you are not a helpless victim of your seemingly irreversible financial problems. You do not need to be held captive by the evil snares of poverty and insufficiency any longer.

There is nothing spiritual in poverty, nothing blessed in not being able to pay your bills, and nothing sacred about tattered clothes. God wants you to live in abundance, and He has given you specific instructions for increasing your finances.

> **Beloved, I wish above all things that thou mayest prosper and be in health, even as thy soul prospereth.**
>
> **3 John 2**

This very day you can start on a Bible-centered plan to improve your financial condition. It will not be through luck. It will not be through inheritance. It will not be through a tremendous return on a financial investment. But, by applying the spiritual laws of abundance which God has given us to follow, you can start yourself on the way to financial prosperity:

1. Give to God cheerfully.

> ...so let him give; not grudgingly, or of necessity: for God loveth a cheerful giver.
>
> **2 Corinthians 9:7**

Give your tithes and offerings (gifts over the tithe) with a cheerful heart.

2. Plant your seeds liberally.

We have already seen that when you sow sparingly, you will reap sparingly. But, when you sow bountifully, you will reap bountifully.

> But remember this — if you give little, you will get little. A farmer who plants just a few seeds will get only a small crop, but if he plants much, he will reap much.
>
> **2 Corinthians 9:6 TLB**

3. Strive to eliminate your debts as soon as possible.

> Owe no man any thing, but to love one another....
>
> **Romans 13:8**

Set specific goals for getting out of debt.

4. Resist impulse buying.

Always seek God's will and guidance in your major purchases.

5. Invest wisely.

Wise counsel in your investment program is recommended. Listen only to qualified and reputable institutions — those which have a stable, long-term financial record, and which are recommended by people you trust. Also avoid "long shots" and "get-rich-quick" schemes.

However, do not fail to realize that throughout Scripture, it is made very clear the best investment you can make to receive a steady and liberal return, an ongoing increase in your finances, is to *invest in the spreading of the Gospel!*

Plant your money-seeds liberally to take the message of salvation to a needy world, and God will see to it that you prosper *now* and in eternity:

> **But he shall receive an hundredfold *now* in this time,…and in the world to come eternal life.**
> **Mark 10:30**

Remember: if you need an increase in your income, simply increase the measure of your giving:

> **…For with the same measure that ye mete withal (measure) it shall be measured to you again.**
> **Luke 6:38**

Lesson 29:
God Cares How Much You Give

If God didn't care how much or how often you give, he would not have included so many instructions in Scripture concerning the methods, the time and the proper attitudes for giving.

He repeatedly gives instructions about giving, including the specific day for giving:

> **Upon the first day of the week let every one**

of you lay by him in store, as God hath prospered him....

1 Corinthians 16:2

God *does* care when you give, and *He cares how much* you give.

But this I say, He which soweth sparingly shall reap also sparingly; and *he which soweth bountifully shall reap also bountifully.*

2 Corinthians 9:6

When Jesus walked on the earth, He watched the people giving their offerings in the temple:

And Jesus sat over against (opposite) the treasury, and beheld how the people cast money into the treasury....

Mark 12:41

Many Christians would prefer to have this scripture taken out of their Bibles, but like it or not, it is there. Jesus sat and watched the people put their money into the offering. And, as we have seen, Jesus was deeply moved by the attitude and the intentions of the giver. The poor widow who sacrificed her two mites was considered by Jesus to be the most generous giver in all the temple, because her gift was extremely large in proportion to her available money supply.

I would like for you to notice that Jesus was moved by the widow's giving. If we only tip God, we probably hope He doesn't notice, but when we get serious about giving and give a substantial portion of our income to the Lord, it is comforting to know that He takes notice and that proper giving is seen by Him.

Never forget, you are literally positioning your heart before God when you participate in an offering to Him. Remember: **For where your treasure is, there will your heart be also** (Luke 12:34).

Are you beginning to grasp the spirit of this matter? God *does* care about your finances! God immediately knows the measure from which you give, when you give, and the attitudes you have as you are giving.

That is not just my opinion; that is what the Word of God says!

So, plant this firmly in your spirit: giving is important to God. He does care how you give, and He does seem to show a partiality toward the cheerful giver!

> **...for God loveth a cheerful giver.**
>
> **2 Corinthians 9:7**

Lesson 30:
Money Is a Spiritual Subject

Well over 20 percent of Holy Scripture concerns money, wealth, finances, property, lands, possessions, tithes and giving. If money is not a spiritual subject, then why is so much said about it in the Bible?

Scripture clearly shows that God wants you to have money, and to be happy with your wealth:

> **The blessing of the Lord, it maketh rich, and he addeth no sorrow with it.**
>
> **Proverbs 10:22**

> **...yea, let them say continually, Let the Lord be magnified, which hath pleasure in the prosperity of his servant.**
>
> **Psalm 35:27**

Scripture gives clear instructions on how to increase your funds:

Give, and it shall be given unto you....
Luke 6:38

Scripture clearly shows that when you give your money, you are performing an *act of sacred worship* to your God!

Bring ye all the tithes into the storehouse, that there may be meat (food) in mine house, and prove (test) me now herewith, saith the Lord of hosts, if I will not open (for) *you* the windows of heaven, and pour you out a blessing, that there shall not be room enough to receive it.
Malachi 3:10

Deuteronomy 26:1-12, plainly states that tithing and offerings are specific worship services before God.

You see, Satan has lied to the Body of Christ, and has somehow convinced us that money is evil — or at least definitely unspiritual. That is a lie!

Money is a spiritual matter.

Money is one of the acceptable scriptural offerings for the worship of the Lord.

Money is an effective tool to help bring the message of salvation to lost souls throughout the world.

Satan has lied to us about money, but when you put your money into use according to the biblical principles, and with a truly scriptural heart, money becomes a very sacred thing.

Money is your life. Each week when you are paid, the paycheck you receive is the company's way of reimbursing you for the part of your life you spent in service to the firm.

Friend, if you are sanctified holy through the blood of Christ, and you give a part of your holy life each week to your employer, then the money he gives you in exchange for your life is *holy money* and represents a portion of your total life.

Lesson 31:
Give, Expecting to Receive

The following statement is probably one of the most shocking and hard-to-believe biblical principles for the Body of Christ to accept: "Give, expecting to receive."

When most Christians give, they sincerely feel they should not expect anything back for what they have given. Inside, they say something like this:

"Lord, I don't want anything in return. I don't expect anything back. I'm just giving because I love You."

Beloved, when you give and expect nothing back, that is well and good and noble, and God will honor your heart — but that is not giving the biblical way!

Here is the godly way to give: Give, *expecting to receive!*

Notice I said that this is "the godly way." When God gave, He gave with definite expectations. For instance, when God created mankind, and gave him life, He *expected to receive* back from man worship, reverence, love, service, obedience, companionship, and ultimately sonship.

Again, when God gave His Son, Jesus, to die for us, He gave Him, expecting to receive sons and daughters in return.

The Word of God is very clear on the fact that giving is irreversibly tied to receiving: **Give, and it shall be given unto you...**(Luke 6:38). Moreover, giving is irreversibly tied to receiving a return on what is given.

> **Be not deceived; God is not mocked: for whatsoever a man soweth, that shall he also reap.**
> **Galatians 6:7**

Once again, let me say that this is not my promise or my idea; it's God's Word!

God promises that when you give your tithes and offerings, He will **open you the windows of heaven, and pour you out a blessing.** (Mal. 3:10). If you have trouble with that concept, take it up with God. It is not John Avanzini's idea; it is God's Word!

Again and again, God says to give, expecting to receive, so you can give even more the next time. *It is a godly way to give, expecting to receive in return.* Giving in expectation of receiving does not make a person selfish. Every informed Christian would gladly give his tithes and offerings just because he loves God and wants to obey His commandments. But God's ways are always better than man's ways. If the Lord did not give back a more abundant return than what was given, where would the money come from to take the Gospel to the world?

You see, God knows what He is doing.

Stop saying that you do not expect anything back from God when you give. That simply is not a biblical statement. Give, expecting to receive, so you can turn right around and be a good steward by giving even more to God's Kingdom work next time.

I have found no limit in God's Word to the abundance that you can have for the Gospel, and for your family — *if* you systematically persist in doing God's will in your finances.

Ten Truths About Money In Summary

I hope by now that you have realized you are reading this book because God wants you to *experience* a major breakthrough in the area of your finances. If you have begun to practice these concepts, God is literally beginning to strategically position you in His end-time harvest plan.

I sincerely pray that you will continue to experience this book, precept upon precept, line upon line. Look upon each new lesson and concept as a precious treasure, and allow the truths in them to become part of your mind. Continue to read each lesson in the morning, and then again in the evening. Feel free to go back as often as you please and reread any lesson that you have already read. That is God's way for you to experience change, transformation, and breakthrough!

Make no mistake about it, *Satan wants you to be poor*. The devil can be much more effective in neutralizing your testimony if you are financially weak and impotent. But, as the final end-time events begin to unfold around you, God wants to arm you with all His spiritual armor, and with the finances you need to effectively bring the message of salvation to a dying world.

In spiritual warfare, money is one of the necessary tools to provide desperately needed Bibles for the entire world. The production and dissemination of evangelistic television programs in many languages demand extensive funding. Even personal evangelism on every continent will be very expensive and will take thousands of times the money currently being allocated to world evangelism. Money is not only a spiritual subject, it is one of *the primary keys* to bringing the Gospel to a lost world.

That's why Satan has tried to make up so many lies about money, and has deceived so many of the saints. The "Ten Truths About Money" you have just studied are intended to shock your mind out of its old ruts and out of the deceptive patterns Satan has used to feed you his mistaken ideas about money. Before you move on to the next section of this book, flip through this section and read the lesson headings again — only this time say them out loud.

Really allow them to settle into your spirit.

Then go back and say them again.

Remember: nothing you can ever do will more dramatically change your financial circumstances than your active *participation in the process* of transforming your mind in the area of finances.

Everything else is easy.

Once you understand that God intends for you to be prosperous, and once you learn how to apply His principles of biblical economics in your life, you are on your way to a financial transformation.

This is not my "pie in the sky" promise to keep you reading — this is God's Word for you:

"Give, and it shall be given unto you."

What a glorious day this is! Scripture teaches us that Satan has been defeated for centuries, but in the area of finances, many of the saints still function as victims instead of victors.

We enthusiastically accept salvation.

We willingly receive the Holy Ghost.

Today, I believe God is "birthing" in you a new understanding about the Gospel, an understanding that involves *accepting God's prosperity for your life*. Not just for material purposes (food, clothing, and housing), but so that you will have "more than enough" to meet your needs and to bring the message of Jesus Christ to a searching world.

Section V:
Five Major Mistakes About Money

Lesson 32: Mistake 1
— The Fear of Money

The world in which you and I live operates according to its own "Golden Rule": *whoever owns the gold makes the rules.*

Did you know the Bible teaches almost the same principle? If you doubt it, read Ecclesiastes 10:19:

> A feast is made for laughter, and wine maketh merry: but *money answereth all things.*

If you don't think that statement is true, just ask a mother who has to buy clothes for three or four children to go to school. Money will answer her problem.

Just ask anyone who is hungry. Recently, someone said to me, "You know, Brother John, money is not very important to me."

"Brother, I know something about you," I replied. "I know you've never been hungry."

For too long the saints of God have accepted Satan's lies, and have acted as though money is something to be "feared." If you are one of those saints, then take these three key scriptures and put them up in a prominent place where you can see them and repeat them out loud every day:

Key scripture 1:

> **But thou shalt remember the Lord thy God: for it is he that giveth thee power to get wealth, that he may establish his covenant....**
>
> **Deuteronomy 8:18**

Key scripture 2:

> **Beloved, I wish above all things that thou mayest prosper and be in health, even as thy soul prospereth.**
>
> **3 John 2**

Key scripture 3:

> **The blessing of the Lord, it maketh rich, and he addeth no sorrow with it.**
>
> **Proverbs 10:22**

You do not need to fear money: finances are not to be feared by those who are faithful. Prosperity is God's desire for you, and as long as you function in accordance with His commandments, you will experience His blessings in your life.

Lesson 33: Mistake 2 — Poverty is Godly

If God's Word commanded us to be poor, we would obey.

But God's Word does not advocate poverty!

Most Christians are operating in a poverty mentality, while the devil's crowd lives the best life possible.

In Ephesians, Paul talks about **...the riches of the glory of his inheritance in the saints** (Eph. 1:18). The Greek word translated **riches** in this verse is *ploutos*. It is a form of a base word meaning to "fill." Its literal meaning is "money, possessions."

Figuratively it refers to "abundance, riches, valuable bestowment."

Our inheritance as sons and daughters of the King of Kings is a life free from want and poverty.

Read carefully what the Scripture says. Our inheritance is "the riches of the glory of his (God's) inheritance." Yet, most of us are settling for the shells while the devil's crowd eats the peanuts.

The earth is *the Lord's!*

God owns the cattle on a thousand hills, but He has never eaten a hamburger! What does He want with all those cows?

They are for us!

Poverty is not godly, and it certainly is not biblical. God wants you and me to open our eyes to see the invisible world — to see the blessings He has in store for us and for all those who love Him:

> According as his divine power hath given unto us *all things that pertain unto life and godliness*, through the knowledge of him that hath called us to glory and virtue.
>
> **2 Peter 1:3**

Does gasoline pertain to life? Do shoes pertain to life? Does food pertain to life? Yes!

You can lay hands on the sick, bind demons, and manifest strong spiritual power, but your Father also knows that you have need of many material things.

It is no surprise to God that your car needs tires.

It is no surprise to God that you need a coat when the temperature is below freezing.

God intends for you to have all your needs supplied according to *His riches* in glory. In Christian circles, poverty may be popular, but it is not a Bible-founded principle. Poverty goes against everything the Bible teaches and finds its roots, causes, and effects in its author, Satan.

Lesson 34: Mistake 3
— The Best Things in Life Are Free

Many times the devil invents a very spiritual-sounding phrase to try to keep the Church weak and floundering. Perhaps one of his most effective lies is: "The best things in life are free."

That simply is not true. The best things in life are not free. Our salvation was not free. God paid the ultimate price for it, the death of His Son, Jesus Christ!

Even Bibles come with a price. They cost money to print. Over the last 2,000 years, literally billions of dollars have been spent so men and women could have the Scriptures in their hands.

Spreading the Gospel costs money. Today, television and satellites are major vehicles to send the Word of God to other lands. Do you know how much it costs to rent just one channel on a satellite for one month? As much as $200,000. The message of the Gospel is the "best thing" the world could possibly have, but it didn't come free to you or me or anyone else! Someone had to pay to get it to us.

The marvelous testimonies you see on your favorite television ministry program, or the wonderful sermon at your local church on Sunday did not come free! The men and women who recorded the message needed money to pay their staff, buy cameras and film, and then purchase air time so you could see the message and be blessed. Your pastor is usually paid, and your church needs light, heat, literature, pews, microphones and many other types of equipment. Somebody must pay for these things.

You see, the best things in life are *not* free. It takes money to print and buy Bibles. It takes money to carry the Gospel to other lands — whether the vehicle is a missionary, a television camera, a crusade or a satellite — they all take money!

Mexico needs the Gospel. India needs the Gospel. China needs the Gospel. Every home in North America needs the Gospel.

And it will take money to get it to them — lots of it.

The best thing in life — the Gospel of Jesus Christ — does not come free!

This is not my idea, and I am not the only one who has discussed it. Many others know the need for money. The Apostle Paul even discussed the need for Christians to come together with the necessary funds to send missionaries to other lands:

> **How then shall they call on him in whom they have not believed? and how shall they believe in him of whom they have not heard? and how shall they hear without a preacher?**
>
> **And how shall they preach, except they be sent?....**
>
> **Romans 10:14,15**

Lesson 35: Mistake 4
— Poverty Will Bring Happiness

Prosperity alone will never make you happy. But, neither will poverty.

We discussed before that rich people commit suicide, take drugs, get drunk, and get divorced. But so do poor people. There is nothing sacred, holy, or happy about being poor. Happiness has absolutely nothing to do with the presence or absence of material things, but unhappiness can come from a lack of certain material necessities, such as food, clothing and housing.

Happiness has to do primarily with the inner man. There's a little person who lives down inside you, and if that person is not happy, neither wealth nor poverty will bring happiness.

Your inner man can only be touched by two forces — Satan or Christ. If Satan controls your inner person, then you will be unhappy. And, if Jesus Christ has possession of your inner man, you will be happy — marvelous and miraculous things will happen to you.

You see, neither money *nor the lack of it* will change your inner man. Being poor will never make you holy or happy.

But, if you are prosperous and have a Christ-controlled inner man, the Spirit of Christ within you will influence the way you spend your wealth. You will meet your own basic needs and wants, and you will support world mission projects, strategic television outreaches, special projects in your local church, and other Gospel outreaches. Your money will bring you happiness because it will be accomplishing God's purpose for giving it to you.

Poverty or wealth will not bring happiness — that comes only from Jesus Christ. But, once you have Jesus Christ as the Lord of your life, you will be able to bring much happiness to the Body of Christ with the money which you supply for the spreading of the Gospel.

So decide now to begin to prosper and be in good health. As you give to God, He will return your money to you so that you can again give to His purposes.

Lesson 36: Mistake 5 — God Does Not Care About Finances

God does care about finances, but not the way the world cares. Remember what we are learning about God: His ways are not the world's ways.

The world's way of looking at a donation or gift is totally different from God's way. In the world, people who give the most money to a charitable project are honored with banquets, special plaques, ceremonial pins, and by the naming of buildings and hospital wings after them. They receive many outward recognitions that set them apart and reward them in accordance with how much they have given.

God takes special notice of finances which are donated, but in a totally different way. We have already talked about the poor widow who gave her two mites. Many others tossed much larger amounts into the treasury, but God honored the widow because she gave a *greater percentage*, or a *greater portion*, of her total finances to Him.

Jesus took very special notice of that widow. He even called the disciples to come and see, and then openly and publicly said to them:

> ...Verily I say unto you, That this poor widow hath cast more in, than all they which have cast into the treasury:
>
> For all they did cast in of their abundance; but she of her want did cast in all that she had, even all her living.
>
> Mark 12:43,44

Notice the difference: the world recognizes how much you *give*. God recognizes how much you *have left after you have given*.

Isn't that comforting? You can depend upon God, because He does care about your finances. The world only cares about how much you give, but God sees not only how much you give but also how much you have left, and He knows how much money you need to meet your needs each day.

As you give to Him and His work, He will take care of you. He will give back to you more than enough to meet your own needs with plenty left over so you can give to His work again.

God cares so much about your finances that if you will become obedient to His instructions in giving and receiving, and release His hand in your finances, He will start to work *immediately* to change your financial situation, and get you out of debt and into abundance.

The best way to get out of debt and financial troubles is by giving to God.

No matter how tight your finances are, or how unscriptural your giving may have been in the past, if you obey God now and give as He tells you to give, your financial problems will become financial blessings! God always gives back to you what you give to Him, and more.

> **Give, and it shall be given unto you; good measure, pressed down, and shaken together, and running over, shall men give into your bosom. For with the same measure that ye mete withal (measure) it shall be measured to you again.**
>
> **Luke 6:38**

Remember: when you give generously to God, He is blessed by what you give and concerned about what you have left. As you give, God will provide you with more than enough to meet all of your needs and wants.

Five Major Mistakes About Money In Summary

Do you know that you live in a controlled shortage?

The diamond mine owners in South Africa meticulously control the number of diamonds which are available each year. They know that diamonds would not be very valuable if *all* the diamonds in the world appeared in the marketplace at the same time. These owners even buy back large quantities of diamonds just to keep the number in circulation low enough to keep the price up.

The entire purpose of the current oil cartel is to regulate and control the flow of oil into each country, so a "glut" (excess supply) never drives down the price of oil, reducing their profits. The world's oil supply is in a constant state of controlled shortage to assure its high price.

Even our food production is in a controlled shortage — just ask any farmer. Even in North America, farmers are told which crops and in what quantity to grow them, as well as what to do with the surplus (the amount the government does not want to circulate to keep prices at a "fair market" price). As a result, millions of bushels of grain are stored, and many times spoil, while some Americans do not have enough to eat.

You see, to the world, the accumulation of money and the maintenance of good, high prices are the main goals.

In your own spiritual walk with your personal finances, you are also living in a controlled shortage. Right now, the mints are making money so fast that the presses have to be oiled continuously to keep them from catching on fire. That is how fast they are producing money. But, most of us are limited to the little bit of cash in our pockets and in our checking accounts — that meager amount someone else decides is enough for us. As long as we keep our "controlled shortage" mentality, we will not see beyond what is in our pocket or bank account.

But, God says that He owns the silver and gold! However, in the natural world today, much of the control of these items is not in the hands of the Christians. Without firing a shot, the saints of God are losing the financial war.

But you can unleash God's power and abundance into your financial affairs and destroy the "controlled shortage" in your life.

> **Now unto him that is able to do exceeding abundantly above all that we ask *or think*, according to the power that worketh in us.**
> **Ephesians 3:20**

Now, all of us know how to ask for some pretty nice things. God tells us to ask, and He says He can even supply beyond what we can think. There is a "controlled shortage" in the pockets of God's children, but we are causing the shortage by our own limited "shortage thinking"! When will we open the eyes of our understanding?

God's storage houses are chock-full to the brim and overflowing with His abundance. He says, "Just ask."

Are you starting to see with spiritual eyes? We talk about "reaching the world" through great technological outreaches. Well, we can't see beyond the limitations of our own pocketbooks. If we are going to properly finance the outreach of the Kingdom of God, then we had better start seeing beyond our own limited supply. We must lift our eyes and look on God's great storage houses. Psalm 84:11 says:

> **For the Lord God is a sun and shield: the Lord will give grace and glory: *no good thing will he withhold from them that walk uprightly*.**

Is money a good thing?

Yes, when it is in the control of an informed child of God!

God wants to bless you with the grace of His salvation. God wants to bless you with good health.

God wants to bless you with the power, the comfort and the gifts of the Holy Ghost.

And, He wants to bless you with abundant finances!

God is not playing games. Now is the time to bring in the end-time harvest, but we cannot do that without equally huge amounts of money to pay for the things necessary to reap that harvest: television cameras, satellite receivers, salaries for the workers, church buildings, missionary outreaches. All that money must come from only one place, and that is from the saints of God who have taken hold of the blessings God intends for their finances.

Pornographic magazine publishers will not finance the end-time harvest.

Big business is not going to pay for it.

But, nevertheless, it will take huge amounts of money — held in the control of God's children — to reap the great end-time harvest which I believe is coming very soon.

It is time for you and me to end the *"controlled shortage mentality."*

Section VI:
The Good Life!

Lesson 37: Should Christians Have Luxuries?

If Lesson 1 of this book had started with this question, I suspect you probably would have answered with a resounding "No!" After all, don't most Christians believe that luxuries are excessive, worldly, and certainly not of God?

But now, I hope that when you read the question, you started your "new mentality" wheels turning, and answered "I'm really not sure," or better yet, "Yes! God wants me to have luxuries."

Let's look at one key example in God's Word to begin to determine an answer to this highly controversial question.

First, let's decide clearly what luxuries are. My dictionary defines the word *luxuries* as "the comforts and beautiful things of life *beyond what are really necessary*." The next definition reads, in part: "costly foods, ... clothing, houses, or furniture; the things a person enjoys, usually very costly and very choice."

For decades Christians have felt that we should have just enough to eat, an inexpensive car to ride in, and the very simplest of clothes. It was considered "holy" to just barely make it. Somehow poverty was thought to be a sign of spirituality or great love for God.

But, Jesus didn't seem to function in that frame of mind. In fact, the first miracle He ever performed was a miracle of luxury! This miracle of luxury was of a material nature. It took place at the marriage feast in Cana, as told in the second chapter of the Gospel of John.

When the hosts of this marriage feast ran out of wine, what did Jesus do? He didn't say, "Well, the guests have had enough; it's time for everyone to go home."

No! He made wine for the people in attendance, and the Apostle John reports that it was the *best* wine. This was one of the luxuries of life.

I think it is very important to note that the first miracle Jesus ever performed was a miracle of luxury, and He did it after everyone had already had plenty of wine to drink.

God does not mind if you have nice things.

Also, of all the possessions Jesus personally owned, the one that the Bible describes was His cloak. It was the finest of coats, so lovely that the soldiers who crucified Him cast lots for it to see who would be fortunate enough to have it.

That is not all!

As you continue this study, you will discover many other similar examples of God's luxurious giving. If God Himself set the pattern, then who are we to change it?

Lesson 38: Is Jesus Against You Having Luxuries?

One day, shortly before His crucifixion, Jesus was having dinner in the home of a Pharisee when a woman brought "an alabaster box of very precious ointment" and anointed Him with it. His disciples saw the action, and said:

> ...To what purpose is this waste?
>
> For this ointment might have been sold for much, and given to the poor.
>
> Matthew 26:8,9

Instead of agreeing with the apostles, Jesus replied:

> ...Why trouble ye the woman? for she hath wrought a good work upon me.
>
> Matthew 26:10

Once again, we see Jesus does not mind nice things. And, as He advised His apostles, He didn't even answer their comments about waste. Instead He commended the woman's actions and called them a "good work."

Jesus appreciated the woman's kindness. In fact, He even prophesied that:

> ...Wheresoever this gospel shall be preached in the whole world, there shall also this, that this woman hath done, be told for *a memorial of her.*
>
> Matthew 26:13

There are no doubt many saints who would like to somehow take these words out of the Scriptures, because they do not line up with *man's* teaching of supposed humility through poverty and insufficiency! Jesus recognized there was enough wealth in the world for everyone, and that it was just fine for the luxurious alabaster ointment to be poured over Him. Jesus appreciated this woman's heart so much that

He ordained that her actions would be remembered right along with the Gospel, as a magnificent "memorial" to her!

Notice, nowhere did Jesus ever memorialize the actions of those who exemplified poverty, lack and insufficiency. But here he memorializes this good deed done to Him with the costly ointment.

Is Jesus against luxuries? The Word of God certainly gives us no indication that He opposed them during His earthly ministry. His own actions seem to indicate He was not against them, so why are so many Christians today against luxuries?

They are against them because they are believing *the mistaken ideas of some preacher* instead of patterning their lives and attitudes after *the* pattern, Jesus Christ. Luxuries are not out of the question for the children of God; but remember: the greatest luxury of all is the precious blood of Jesus which was poured out without limit for all the world.

Please remember also that we should never leave the precious Gospel unpreached so that we can have our luxuries. By now you should be convinced that if you give generously into the preaching of the Gospel, God will not withhold any good thing from you.

Lesson 39: You Can Have the Good Things in Life

My life began to change dramatically when I started to believe God's promises. You see, it doesn't really matter how expensive clothing gets, or how high the price of groceries soars, because God says

He will take care of us if we are taking care of those ministries that are preaching the Gospel around the world.

It is very simple. If you believe and trust God, then you will give to His work just as the Scriptures teach. And, here is the good news of what is promised in return for your giving:

> **But my God shall supply all your need** *according to his riches* **in glory by Christ Jesus.**
> Philippians 4:19

Notice, this verse does not say that God will supply these good things *out of* His riches in glory, but rather that He will supply them *in accordance with* His riches in glory. That means that God plans to supply you according to His riches in glory, according to the good things He enjoys in heaven.

Of course, we know that heaven is not a *simple place*; it is not a *poverty-ridden* place. Heaven's throne is not made out of wood and plaster and thread-bare upholstery.

The Apostle John surely isn't describing a slum or a secondhand store when he gives us the description of God's riches in glory:

> **And the building of the wall of it was of jasper: and the city was pure gold, like unto clear glass.**
>
> **And the foundations of the wall of the city were garnished with all manner of precious stones. The first foundation was jasper; the second, sapphire; the third, a chalcedony; the fourth, an emerald;**
>
> **The fifth, sardonyx: the sixth, sardius; the seventh, chrysolite; the eighth, beryl; the ninth, a**

topaz; the tenth, chrysoprasus; the eleventh, a jacinth; the twelfth, an amethyst.

And the twelve gates were twelve pearls; every several gate was of one pearl: and the street of the city was pure gold, as it were transparent glass.

Revelation 21:18-21

God enjoys good things, and He said He will supply our needs in that same fashion, "according to His riches in glory." (Phil. 4:19) God wants you to have good things.

Think with me. Suppose you were doing well and prospering, and your son or daughter became a partner with you. Suppose he or she pleased you very much by being a great worker in the family business. Would you live in a mansion in the best part of town and allow your child to live in a cheap apartment in the slums? Would you enjoy riches, but expect him or her to barely get by?

Certainly not.

Scripture tells us that if we — as human beings — know how to give good gifts to our children, how much more will God give His children good things.

If ye then, being evil, know how to give good gifts unto your children: how much more shall your heavenly Father give....

Luke 11:13

Lesson 40:
God Wants You Always Abounding!

God does not talk about barely enough in even one place in Scripture. The psalmist David wrote of the Lord:

> **Thou preparest a table** (a banquet) **before
> me in the presence of mine enemies: thou anoin-
> test my head with oil;** *my cup runneth over.*

> **Surely goodness and mercy shall follow me
> all the days of my life: and I will dwell in the
> house of the Lord for ever.**
>
> **Psalm 23:5,6**

Are you beginning to grasp the desire of God?
He wants you to sit at a banquet table. He wants you
anointed with costly oil. He wants your cup to over-
flow with good things. He wants goodness and
mercy in your life!

There's no talk in the Bible about running out,
or running short, or doing without, or not having
enough food to eat. God talks about abundance. He
talks about always abounding in the magnificent
things He has created for us!

How many times have you stood in a store and
weighed the difference between a bad suit or a good
suit, a cheap dress or a well-made one? How many
times have you bought a poor pair of jeans, instead of
a pair that would last? How many times have you
thought, "As Christians, we just can't have the best"?

I've got a shocking statement for you: *God
wants you to have the best!*

Look at the type of clothes Jesus wore. When
He was crucified, the soldiers tore up the garments of
the other two men, but when it came to Jesus, they
did not tear up his cloak:

> **Then the soldiers, when they had crucified
> Jesus, took his garments...and also his coat: now
> the coat was without seam, woven from the top
> throughout.**

> They said therefore among themselves, Let
> us not rend (tear) it, but cast lots for it, whose it
> shall be....
>
> John 19:23,24

The coat Jesus wore was very fine indeed, so
fine that the soldiers did not want to destroy it. Jesus
wore good things, and He wants you to pattern yourself after Him.

The Apostle Paul also had a fine cloak, fine
enough for him to specifically ask Timothy to bring it
all the way from Troas to the city of Rome. It must
have been very valuable to warrant asking Timothy
to inconvenience himself by keeping it with him all
that way:

> The cloke that I left at Troas with Carpus,
> when thou comest, bring with thee....
>
> 2 Timothy 4:13

Lesson 41: A Half-Truth Will Not Set You Free

Only the whole truth will set you free.

Most Christians know half the truth. They
know that Jesus commanded us to give up all we
have and follow Him. And that's good teaching. I
teach that. I preach that. But, there's a second part to
that truth — and only when you understand the second part will you really be set free.

You see, Jesus *did* say to give up all and follow
Him, but He also said that if we would do that, He
would give back to us a hundredfold here and now.

In this lifetime.

Now, a lot of people who hear that statement
will say, "Brother John, I just don't believe that."

Well, whether anyone believes it or not doesn't change the fact that Jesus said it!

> ...Verily I say unto you, There is no man that hath left house, or brethren, or sisters, or father, or mother, or wife, or children, or lands, for my sake, and the gospel's,
>
> But *he shall receive an hundredfold now in this time,* houses, and brethren, and sisters, and mothers, and children, and lands, with persecutions; and in the world to come eternal life.
>
> Mark 10:29,30

There it is in black and white! You will receive a hundredfold return *now! In this time* — not after you die and are in heaven. Houses. Lands. Brothers. Sisters. Surely we can see that. Jesus wants you to give all you have for Him, but only so He can give it back to you.

God does not want you poor or homeless or without family. He only wants you to give up those things — to Him — so He can multiply them back to you.

Now, this doesn't always call for deeding all your property to the Church. But, it does mean giving God control of all your possessions. Very seldom have I ever heard of God asking anyone to sell everything and give to His work, but sometimes He does. One time He asked my wife and me to give up our house, and we did. He then immediately put us into a new house we liked even better, and we began to experience more abundance than we had ever thought possible. *But, be very careful in these decisions, as they can bring ruin into your life if they are made without God's specific instructions.*

Lesson 42: Release It All, and You'll Get It All Back

When you release everything to the Lord, He promises to return it all to you abundantly. That is the promise of the tenth chapter of Mark, verses 29 and 30.

God *made the promise,* now He is waiting for His people to grasp His mentality in relation to abundance, and to stop being cheated out of what is potentially theirs.

You see, when you release control of your possessions unto the Lord, you do not give up a thing. Read Mark 10, verses 29 and 30, again. It deals with the things we understand: houses, lands and families. Don't turn a deaf ear to what God wants you to hear in this passage. Do not let Satan lie to you even one more day by telling you that it is "holy" to be poor.

In the deepest sense, to be *poor* means to be "powerless." If Satan can keep the saints trembling in shoes full of holes, living in rented houses, and barely able to make payments and buy groceries, then he can effectively stop the spreading of the Gospel to the world. Every satellite network, every Christian television station, every soulwinning ministry, every evangelist, every Christian writer, every teacher, every Christian radio show needs money to carry on an effective Gospel outreach. So you can see why Satan wants to keep the saints poor.

In Mark 10:29 and 30, God is not talking about a poverty Gospel. Nor is He talking about only religious things. He is talking about houses and lands!

Mark 10:29 and 30 is God's promise — not man's. Man would never make such a promise. Only God has the resources to back it up.

God wants you to release everything — not so you will not be poor, but so He can make you far richer than you were before!

That is God's way of preparing you for your dynamic part in the financing of His great end-time harvest!

Lesson 43: How to Get the Good Life Going (Part 1)

Most people think the "good life" involves material things — fancy houses, nice cars, expensive boats, and elaborate seven-course dinners. Those things are nice, but they are not the "good life." You see, the good life comes from within:

> **Beloved, I wish above all things that thou mayest prosper and be in health, even as thy soul prospereth.**
>
> **3 John 2**

Both the conditions for prosperity and the conditions for health, are in the well-being and the prosperity of the inner man. The good things in life do not come from the outside; they come from within and go to the outside man.

When I write about the "good life," many inattentive Christians misunderstand what I am talking about. They think I am talking about a carnal type of lifestyle, but I'm not. What I'm saying is that if you will get "the good life" inside of you, you can't help but get your life right on the outside.

121

The good life does not depend upon the neighborhood you live in nor the price of your home. The good life depends on what is going on inside of you. Remember: it is from the inside out that the good things within you will begin to manifest themselves. The luxuries of life grow forth from the inside.

Paul was able to turn a dungeon into a palace:

> ...I have learned, in whatsoever state I am, therewith to be content.
>
> **Philippians 4:11**

History tells us of many kings who did just the opposite; they turned their palaces into dungeons — because they did not have the truth within themselves.

> For I rejoiced greatly, when the brethren came and testified of the truth that is in thee, even as thou walkest in the truth.
>
> **3 John 3**

John did not get excited when he heard that someone had gotten a new home or fancy clothes. He rejoiced when he learned that "the truth" was in those around him. For he knew that as their souls prospered, they would materially prosper and be in health.

When you operate in the truth, then you will also operate in prosperity.

Once these truths of prosperity are in your spirit, then you need to start walking in them. When that happens, you will prosper in your body, your spirit, your soul, as well as in your financial matters.

Lesson 44: How to Get the Good Life Going (Part 2)

When I talk about "the good life," please remember that I am not talking about cars, houses, vacations, fancy food, and expensive entertainment.

Cars will wear out. A house can soon become part of a slum district. The taste of fancy food lasts only a few minutes. Vacations are quickly forgotten. All of these things are nice to have in your life, but they are *not* "the good life."

If you really have the good life, your quality of life will transcend the natural and focus on the spiritual. The Scriptures tell us:

> ...Take no thought for your life, what ye shall eat; neither for the body, what ye shall put on.
>
> The life is more than meat, and the body is more than raiment.
>
> Luke 12:22,23

God wants you to eat, and He wants you to have fine clothes, *but* do not be anxious for them! Do not hunger after them; do not make them the lords of your life! In these verses, Jesus is not talking about depriving yourself of food and other nice things. He simply is asking that you keep your priorities straight.

> But rather seek ye the kingdom of God; and *all these things* shall be added unto you.
>
> Luke 12:31

Are you seeing the truth in this matter? Your life is more than food, drink, a nice house and vacations. Your good life *starts* when you seek first God's Kingdom and God's way, when you literally put

God's Kingdom first. When you begin to live totally in Christ, understanding that you are God's temple, the dwelling place of the Most High, then you will have nice clothes, a good car and a beautiful home. Yes, all of these things will be added unto you.

You see, it is a matter of priority.

When you put the things that pertain to Jesus in first place, your life is going to count; you cannot help but experience the good life, and *all* of your needs will be met.

The Gospel of Jesus Christ has never been and never will be a Gospel of deprivation! God does not want to deprive you of the things you need to live, and to live abundantly. All God wants you to do is make sure you seek Him first; then, all the other things will be added unto you.

When good times and the good life come to you, do not stop seeking the Lord, for as surely as you do, those things that you need that were so richly added to you will begin to fall away.

Lesson 45: You Are Halfway There!

If you have made it this far through this study, smile! You will complete the rest of this life-transforming process. You see, in the first forty-five lessons you have read and considered dynamic biblical economic truths that may have totally shocked and upset you, as well as challenged you to rethink what the Gospel says about the riches of this planet. If you have read them with an open mind, then I believe you are being changed. You are seeing that poverty is not a holy condition instituted by God for His special people. Rather, it is just the opposite!

You and I serve a God of abundance!

The Word of God declares Him to be so. Our God first cares about our inner man. He wants us to walk in His image and in His commandments and precepts.

Once you master that concept, "all these things" will be added unto you. This will not happen just because you need a nice car, or because you desperately hunger after the best house on the block, but because God knows your heart, knows He can trust your stewardship, and wants to give you good things.

Jesus created "the best" wine for his contemporary friends.

Jesus allowed the anointing with expensive alabaster oil.

Jesus wore a cloak so fine that the soldiers did not dare to tear it up.

Why?

Was it because Jesus felt that good wine and expensive oil and fine cloaks were His life? Of course not. These things were not a priority in His life, but as long as serving His father was His main priority, "all these things" were added to Him.

God owns all the silver and the gold (Haggai 2:8), so it is no big deal for Him to give some of these things to His servants. This is especially true when He knows their hearts to be pure and knows they are not more "anxious" and excited for these material things than they are for Him and His Kingdom.

Continue your study. Your mind transformation is critical in determining how you will spend the remaining years on this planet. It is also critical to how quickly we will begin to reap the end-time harvest for Jesus Christ.

It is only when the saints grasp these principles of biblical economics that there will be the ability and the funds to operate full-time Christian television, the wealth needed for Christian satellites to beam the Gospel around the world, the money needed to send preachers to foreign lands, and the resources required to finance every other good work God wants done in these great end times.

You can be sure that the wicked will not carry out this vital work; it is up to you and me to grasp God's life-changing principles and to apply them in our individual lives!

Lesson 46: Making Your Life Rich for God

Make no mistake about it — you and I are living in the end times. We are down to the final harvest. Yet, look around you. The Church of Jesus Christ does not have enough tools to bring in the harvest or enough storage bins to house them if we did. There are more than two and one-half billion souls out there who are still waiting to hear about our Jesus — and we don't have the proper funds to send them the preachers, or to beam them the television programs so they can hear the precious Gospel.

Are millions of people going to hell because God does not provide us with the resources to reach them?

Nonsense.

They are going to hell because the saints of God have not learned to lay hold of the resources that God has already provided!

Yes, God wants you to abound.

Yes, God wants you to be prosperous.

Yes, God wants you to have control over great wealth.

Who else can He trust? Who else will give to bring in the Kingdom? It will not be the multi-millionaire rock stars who sing satanic songs. It won't be the pornographers who make billions of dollars by shooting indecent pictures of little children. It won't be the drug dealers who are daily destroying the lives of so many of our precious teenagers and young adults. Surely, it will not be the liquor manufacturers.

God wants *you* in abundance because only the saints of God will take the prosperity that God has so abundantly given them and *use it* as good stewards, for His glory, and for the salvation of millions of dying souls.

Remember: God has given you the ability to prosper, and with the proper use of that prosperity, God has the ability to reach a dying world with the good news of the Gospel.

Do you understand? We need to circle the globe with the news that the King is coming, and that because of His death for them on the cross, men and women do not have to fear His coming.

I am not talking to you about another "O God, bless me" club. No. I am talking about an "O God, bless me so I can give to help bring in this end-time harvest" club. That's the "club" that will make a difference in our world.

If you and I keep leading our lives according to our old concepts, our old ideas about money and prosperity, then there is no way we will ever reach the lost. It will take a *breakthrough* — in our lives, and in the lives of thousands of other saints — before we will fully experience God's abundance and begin to reach the world.

The Good Life
In Summary

Most Christians do not have an agricultural mentality. They read a book like this, get all excited, go to church on Sunday and give an offering to God, then wake up Monday morning complaining:

"Hey, Brother John, I gave, but it didn't work."

When I hear these folks complaining, I tell them, "Then maybe you should quit serving God."

Naturally, they become very upset. "No. No. I love God. I believe in God. Why do you say such a thing, Brother John?"

"Well, if you believe in God, do you believe in His Word?"

Again, they become rather upset. "Yes, of course I do."

"Then wait," I reply. "Whatever you have planted will come up."

You see, giving to God is like a farmer planting

seed. The farmer does not wake up the next morning after planting the seed to run out to his field, yelling: "It didn't work! It didn't work! My wheat seed didn't come up."

Today, you and I function in an industrial mentality. Everything is instant. Instant printing. Instant fried chicken. Instant banking.

But, the principles of biblical economics are agricultural, farming principles, not industrial principles.

When you sow, you will reap. Not tomorrow, but in due season.

It takes faith and patience to bring these God-given principles to their fullest potential. Plant your seed regularly. At first your sowing will look futile. But, there will come a day when you will have many money seeds of prosperity planted. All of a sudden the harvest will begin to come in such abundance that you will have more than enough!

You must have a farm mentality to understand this principle of sowing and reaping, because that is the way God sends His riches back to us. We plant, and in due season, we harvest.

When I was on a drive through South Africa, I noticed fields of orange-colored dirt stretching for miles in every direction. The fields had been plowed, the ground had been broken up, but there were no crops. I asked my companion to explain the empty fields:

"Those are wheat fields," he told me. "They are waiting for rain."

You see, the seed was in the ground. The fields were already planted, but they were just waiting for rain. When the rain came, it turned those bare hillsides into giant wheat fields producing an abundant harvest!

God has placed in your hands the seeds you need to sow in order to become prosperous. Here they are:

> **But thou shalt remember the Lord thy God: for it is he that giveth thee power to get wealth, *that* he may establish his covenant which he sware unto thy fathers, as it is this day.**
>
> **Deuteronomy 8:18**

God has given you (you already have it!) the *power* to get wealth so that His covenant can be established on earth. But you must use that power with a farmer's mentality. God is not the great "spiritual slot machine in the sky." You do not put in a hundred dollars and instantly get back a thousand. No, you plant a hundred dollars into God's work and let that seed grow and mature and develop so that "in due season" God will return to you many times what you have planted.

When He returns the harvest, go ahead and eat some of the seed. Go ahead and buy a nice car or a new suit, or whatever you desire. Just be sure you save enough seed to abundantly plant again, to put *more money-seeds* into the Gospel, so *God can return to you* even more of His abundance to plant and reap again in constantly increasing harvests for His end-time work.

Section VII:
The Abundance of God!

Lesson 47:
Creation...in Abundance

We serve an abundant God. His creation is in abundance all around us: abundant water, land, mountains, animals, plants, trees, insects, and much more. It only makes sense that He would desire for our lives to abound "exceeding abundantly" too. The Word of God agrees:

> Now unto him that is able to do exceeding abundantly *above all that we ask or think,* according to *the power that worketh in us,*
>
> Unto him be glory in the church by Christ Jesus throughout all ages, world without end. Amen.
>
> **Ephesians 3:20,21**

There are three very critical points contained in this scripture:

First, God not only wants to give us more than we can ask for. He clearly states that He wants to give us more than we can even think about! It is difficult enough for us to understand God giving us more than we can ask for; but even when we stretch our imagination as far as it will go, we still come short of God's desire for us. Yet, He takes us far beyond our desires, all the way to the incomprehensible measure of *more than we can imagine!*

Second, God wants to give us this unlimited blessing "according to the power that worketh in us." Our relationship with God is critical here. God's *promises* will operate through us only to the degree that we allow His *power* to operate in us. We must be totally submissive to His will in our lives if we are to break into the wonderful realm of "above all that we (can) think!"

Third, we see the true purpose of this abundance: "Unto Him be glory!" Abundance above all we ask or think is primarily to bring glory to God. We cannot effectively penetrate our community for God from a position of poverty or selfishness. Contrary to the beliefs of many Christians, God intends abundance for you and me, so we will not be hindered from bringing glory to Him. Remember: this realm of more than we can ask or think belongs to those who seek His glory, not their own.

When you walk in the abundance of God, and go beyond simply having your needs met, you can do some powerful and wonderful things for the Kingdom of God. You can more easily further God's plan when you can get past basic needs such as rent, groceries, utilities, and car payments, and enter into a dimension of more than you can ask or think. In that realm there are more than enough resources available for all the ministries God lays on your heart.

God wants to give you more than you can ask, more than you can think, because His plan for you is infinitely greater than you can ask or imagine!

Most Christians cannot think in this realm. They have a hard time believing that God wants to use them in financing the end-time harvest because the devil has crippled their divine imagination with thoughts of impossibility and insufficiency.

Now, by faith you can break out of the devil's insufficiency thinking, and God will open new visions of abundance that exceed all you can ask or think. God wants you to flourish in His abundance so you will have more than enough to finance the end-time harvest.

Lesson 48:
Walking...in Abundance

How do you start to walk in abundance?

You have already taken *the first step:*

You now know that you know that you know that God intends abundance for His children.

Once you *know* that God desires abundance for you, and *more than you can think,* then you are ready to take the *second step:*

Right now, form an effective giving and receiving covenant with God. Raise your hands and pray this prayer out loud to the Lord:

"Dear Lord, I sincerely desire to give an ever-increasing portion of wealth to You for the financing of Your great end-time harvest. Today, I solemnly pledge to become much more involved in the spreading of the Gospel by starting Your biblical seeding process in my life now. I will begin by faithfully giving $_____ (weekly, monthly) into Your work. (State an amount — it should be over the amount of your tithe.)

"Lord, beginning today, by faith, I am planting these money-seeds to start Your flow of abundance in my life. I promise that as You multiply a money harvest back to me, I will always reinvest a generous portion into the spreading of Your Gospel.

"Thank You, Lord, for revealing these biblical principles of economics to me. I am now determined to unleash these bold new principles into my own life. I thank You now, Lord, for Your abundance which this positive action on my part will bring to pass soon. Amen."

Now take the critical *third step:*

Exercise the covenant. Not only must you *know* God's principles of biblical economics, and make a strong *covenant* with God, you *must faithfully exercise* this covenant; you must now put these principles to work.

Begin giving today, and God will begin blessing and returning to you larger and larger amounts of wealth for you to liberally reinvest into the Gospel ministry.

Give, and it shall be given unto you....
Luke 6:38

There is (he) that scattereth, and yet increaseth; and there is (he) that withholdeth more than is meet (fitting), but it tendeth to poverty.

The liberal soul shall be made fat: and he that watereth shall be watered also himself.
Proverbs 11:24,25

Start being a great receiver by giving generously to the Lord's work right now.

Give to your local church. Give to Christian television. Give to those great ministries God puts on your heart. Always give remembering that your increase does not come from the specific ministry you give to. You are really giving to God, and He has no limit on the ways He will choose to give funds back to you.

Lesson 49:
Prosperity...in Abundance

God's thoughts are not our thoughts. In the natural realm, the proper way to achieve abundance is to keep all the wealth we can, carefully tucking it away in a safe place, and drawing a moderate rate of interest so that it can gradually grow into even more wealth.

But that is not God's plan for the greatest increase in wealth!

In God's Word, we read that we must first give away that which we want to accumulate. If you desire abundance in finances, you must give away a part of your finances. Paul wrote about this principle in Philippians 4:15-17:

> **Now ye Philippians know also, that in the beginning of the gospel, when I departed from Macedonia, no church communicated with me as *concerning giving and receiving, but ye only.***

> **For even in Thessalonica ye sent once and again unto my necessity.**

> **Not because I desire a gift: but I *desire fruit* (finances) *that may abound to your account.***

To flourish in God's prosperity and bask in His abundance, you must first begin to give away, creating a new life-giving flow to your finances. Stagnant finances cannot draw new money to you. Remember: Paul said that giving and receiving are inter-related and interdependent upon each other. I know by now that this doesn't seem contradictory to you. Surely you are beginning to realize the true meaning of this passage:

> **For my thoughts are not your thoughts, neither are your ways my ways, saith the Lord.**
>
> **For as the heavens are higher than the earth, so are my ways higher than your ways, and my thoughts than your thoughts.**
>
> **Isaiah 55:8,9**

Unfortunately, even with this clear disclosure of God's viewpoint, most preachers in the various Christian churches are not thinking the thoughts of God on this subject. For so long, most of our church leaders have preached that it is wrong to seek prosperity, although these same church leaders often have no problem befriending and giving special attention to the few saints who have prosperity and abundance.

But these thoughts are not God's. In Scripture, He plainly declares:

> **But thou shalt remember the Lord thy God: for it is he that giveth thee power to get wealth, that he may establish his covenant which he sware unto thy fathers, as it is this day.**
>
> **Deuteronomy 8:18**

If God did not desire for you to prosper, He would not have given you the power to get wealth.

But don't get upset if your friends and business acquaintances don't instantly begin to put into practice these wonderful new principles of abundance. Remember, God's thoughts are surely not man's thoughts.

The Apostle John prayed two thousand years ago that you would receive God's best:

> **Beloved, I wish above all things that thou mayest prosper and be in health, even as thy soul prospereth.**
>
> **3 John 2**

Lesson 50:
Abound in Faithfulness

A faithful man shall abound with blessings....

Proverbs 28:20

Isn't that a wonderful verse of Scripture? But, what must we do to be considered faithful? If we want to become faithful, we must first promise to be faithful to something. You see, not until we make a promise, and then keep it, have we proven ourselves to be faithful.

Think back to Lesson 48. In that lesson, you promised God to begin planting a specific amount of money into the Gospel. Now, as you faithfully keep that promise, God will consider you to be a faithful person, and He will allow your life to begin to abound with ever-increasing blessings.

Traditionally we have been taught false concepts concerning the blessings which are to abound in our lives. We have been led to believe that the blessings which God promises are only *spiritual* blessings, or blessings which pertain to our spiritual relationship with God — surely they are not financial or material blessings!

The context of this verse alone quickly shows us that the blessings of the faithful men are material and financial. Notice this verse:

> **He that tilleth his land shall have plenty of bread: but he that followeth after vain persons shall have poverty enough.**
>
> **Proverbs 28:19**

There is no question that God wants us to have spiritual blessings; but He also desires, with just as much fervor, that we "have plenty of bread," a symbol of all our material needs. He is not just talking about spiritual blessings — He is talking about basic needs and wants.

Notice that those who are not faithful, who follow after vain persons, or operate a futile plan, shall be poor. When God speaks here of abounding in blessings, the context of this passage indicates that He is talking about much more than spiritual benefits. He is referring to bread for the table, a car for transportation, a home for shelter, and finances to reach a dying world.

If you are *faithful* in keeping your promises to God, then He will be faithful in keeping His promises to you. Remember: He said in Luke 6:38 that if you give, it will be given back to you in greater abundance. That is God's promise for the faithful man or woman.

Be faithful in your pledges to God. Give as much as you promised, and even more, and give it when you said you would. As you obey this principle of biblical economics, God will be faithful to His promises and abundantly bless you.

Lesson 51:
Poverty Is Not Godly

As you read this book you may be living in poverty or great need right now. You may be in a financial wilderness, and it must almost crush your heart to read page after page about the abounding prosperity of Jesus Christ.

I do not want to hurt you with this message, and neither does God. He wants you to abound! So, let's look at a situation of deep poverty that was changed forever by the same truths I have been teaching you in lesson after lesson in this book.

In the eighth chapter of 2 Corinthians, we read that the church of Macedonia was in *deep, deep poverty.* They were so poor that when they put together a financial gift for the Gospel ministry, they had to beg the Apostle Paul, who knew of their "great trial of affliction," and "their deep poverty," to receive it: **Praying (beseeching) us with much intreaty that we would receive the gift...**(2 Cor. 8:4). Yet, because *that church understood the principles of biblical economics*, it prospered so much that the testimony was used to encourage other churches to give.

This pattern takes place throughout God's Word. We've already seen the example of the widow of Zarephath in 1 Kings, chapter 17. She was in deep poverty until she cast off fear and decided to give to God's prophet. When she gave of her food, she became a prosperous woman, with more than enough to meet her own needs.

If poverty were God's will for His children, then when they were deeply into poverty, He surely would not bring his faithful servants out of their circumstances! If it were godly to be poor, God would not have blessed the church at Macedonia so greatly that they **...abounded unto the riches of their liberality** (2 Cor. 8:2).

If poverty were godly, then God would not have given the widow of Zarephath so much that she and her household **...did eat many days. And the barrel of meal wasted not** (was not used up), **neither did the cruse of oil fail...**(1 Kings 17:15,16).

If you are in need and do not have enough to eat or meet your daily needs, then by all means follow the principles of biblical economics which the widow of Zarephath and the church at Macedonia followed:

> **The liberal soul shall be made fat: and he that watereth shall be watered also himself.**
> **Proverbs 11:25**

Remember: God can change your poverty to prosperity, even when you are in deep poverty or down to your last few crumbs. He did it in Bible days, and He will do it for you today.

Lesson 52:
Giving...in Abundance

Right now, you may consider yourself to be a fairly generous giver. You probably are faithful with your tithe, and even give generous offerings when prompted by a well-presented need, or moved upon by the Holy Spirit.

But I want you to enter a whole new dimension of giving and receiving. I want you to experience a bold new realm far beyond what now seems substantial to you.

You see, your giving horizon — the highest, greatest and most blessed experience of giving and receiving you can imagine now — is merely the starting point for a whole new giving experience that is beginning to take form in your spirit today.

Realize that the world is laid off in strata – actual layers of awareness in potential for accomplishment. Now we all know that Satan is trying to keep us from rising above our current level of giving. He wants to keep us in a low level of awareness, far short of what God intends for us, and far short of what you and I desire to attain.

But now is the strategic time for you to make up your mind you are going to think some bold new thoughts, and literally make some new financial breakthroughs.

When I was going to Bible college, once a month I went down to the government welfare office in Springfield, Missouri, and got my box of surplus commodity cheese, government Spam, and rolled oats. The first thing I ate was the cheese. Then the Spam. And, finally, for the last 28 days of the month, I ate awful-tasting rolled oats. Then one day, I realized that most folks were eating better than I was.

They were simply living on another economic level, a financially superior level, right there in the same town. I came to find out there was a crowd of people who were passing down to me the cheese and meat they didn't want!

You see, there are different strata in life. As long as Satan can keep you from climbing out of the stratum you are presently in, he can keep you from having the surplus you need to give to the preaching of the Gospel.

We do not have to wait for some millionaire to go out and get saved to fund God's end-time harvest. The truth of the matter is that when you fully realize the new level of abundance God has for you, and when you realize you can rise up out of the dimension you are in (even if your current status feels like abundance now), you can reach a far more prosperous stratum.

No matter what level you are currently in, it is time to move into a new dimension of abundance. Remember: God has a divine plan for your life, and you can be sure it isn't a cheap, second-class plan. Begin now to prayerfully elevate your thoughts and your finances to a new dimension, asking God to guide you into a new level of plenty.

Remember: you are being changed from glory to glory, or literally from one financial level to a new, higher one. God wants you to go from glory to glory in your finances, so you can consistently increase the amount you give to preach His Gospel throughout the world.

Lesson 53: How Much Does It Cost To Live in Heaven?

How much do you think it will cost to live in heaven for one year? Will we have to buy food? Is rent high there? Will there be doctor bills?

Of course not! Everyone knows that in heaven there will be no need for money to pay for houses, lands or material possessions. We will not need money to pay rent on our heavenly mansions. We will not need money to repair our celestial harps. Money simply will have no value or purpose in heaven.

If this is the case, then let me ask you a much more serious question. Why does the Bible speak of an increase in our money and material wealth and of becoming rich by the blessings of God? Why does the Bible talk about prosperity at all?

Obviously, material blessings are of no value in heaven; they will be completely worthless once we enter the pearly gates. Surely God knows that money, wealth, and prosperity have to do with activity going on right now on this earth. Prosperity, money, and wealth are to be used in this realm.

Listen carefully to the words of Jesus as He promises increase of goods beyond our wildest dreams, not after we get to heaven, but right here and now:

> ...There is no man that hath left house, or brethren, or sisters, or father, or mother, or wife, or children, or lands, for my sake, and the gospel's,
>
> But he shall receive *an hundredfold now in this time,* houses, and brethren, and sisters, and mothers, and children, and lands,...and in the world to come eternal life.
>
> **Mark 10:29,30**

Houses and lands will have no value in eternity. The only place a new house will mean anything to you is *"now in this time!"* Such things have no value in heaven!

Now, granted, God is deeply concerned about your spiritual blessings. But always remember: He is also vitally concerned about your material blessings *now,* in this life.

Please keep the new thoughts you are gaining in their proper perspective with the Word. This is probably a good time to remember once again Deuteronomy 8:18:

> **But thou shalt remember the Lord thy God: for it is he that giveth thee power to get wealth, that he may establish his covenant which he sware unto thy fathers, as it is this day.**

Houses, lands, money, wealth — all of these come to the generous giver of the Gospel, so he or she can give again even more generously to reach the world with the Gospel of the Kingdom of God.

Lesson 54
God Is the Author of Abundance

God wants you to abound, and it is *His blessings* that enable you to accumulate wealth. Here is a *key principle* in biblical economics:

> **The blessing of the Lord, it maketh rich, and he addeth no sorrow with it.**
>
> > **Proverbs 10:22**

God is the author of your abundance; it is part of being blessed by Him. In the Scriptures He has laid down a firm foundational plan to teach you and me *how* to become rich, without sorrows! (Keep in mind that these are God's words, not the words of a man.)

But why has God given us this clear plan for increasing in wealth? Surely, it is not just so we can buy a nice home and drive a new car (although God is not opposed to our having good things).

God's basic desire for us is that we grow beyond simply being blessed, and become a blessing to others.

In Romans 12, verses 6 and 8, we see that giving is a spiritual gift, and that giving liberally to finance the end-time harvest of souls, will bless people in precisely the same way as prophecy, teaching, exhortation or even speaking in tongues:

> **Having then gifts differing according to the grace that is given to us, let us use them: if prophecy, let us prophesy in proportion to our faith....**
>
> **...he who gives, (let him do it) with liberality....**
>
> **Romans 12:6,8** NKJ

We continuously hear about the gift of prophecy. The gift of teaching. The gift of exhortation. The gift of tongues. But, when was the last time you heard a sermon on the gift of giving? But it is there, in black and white, in the twelfth chapter of Romans, and God has given it to us.

Virtually every great work of God has to have a *faithful group of ministers behind it*, people who *minister with their finances*. But surely by now it is becoming clear that you will need "more than enough" if you are to have a giving ministry. That is why God is the author of abundance: *His blessing* can make you rich, without sorrow.

Let's be realistic. You cannot operate in an effective giving ministry from poverty or want or shortage or insufficiency. Remember: the only way out of the four inhibitors of prosperity — poverty, want, shortage, and insufficiency — is generous giving. Remember, too: whatever you give to God will always be given back to you.

Be faithful over a little, and God will give you a lot to be faithful over. If you exercise faithfulness and patience, eventually, you will find yourself in the *ministry of finances,* and you will become a banker for God!

The Abundance of God!
In Summary

I would have never been filled with the Holy Spirit if I had stopped to think about it. You see, everything that was dear to me was on the line, including possibly my marriage! If you marry a girl who doesn't know about or believe in speaking in tongues, and she wakes up one morning and catches you in a corner speaking in tongues, you could have serious marriage problems!

There came a moment, however, when I had to say, "Yes, the fullness of the Holy Spirit is of God, and I want that *power!*" I took it before I could reason it out with my traditional, doctrinal mentality and talk myself out of it.

In this book you are receiving great amounts of information, much of which you have never heard before. But, believe me, you will not have a breakthrough, or receive all that God has for you in the area of your finances, until you reach out and take it!

> **And from the days of John the Baptist until now the kingdom of heaven suffereth violence, and *the violent take it by force.***
>
> **Matthew 11:12**

The kingdom of heaven is taken by force. The violent men of this verse do not wait around until someone cuts them a small slice of heaven; they take it by force themselves. They press upon and lay hold of it. They put their hands out before anyone else and grab for what they want. That is the new attitude the children of God must have in their finances.

You cannot enter into a new dimension of prosperity by being passive. It takes aggressiveness. You must violently snatch your mind out of the ruts of your old thinking, and with deliberate force press into the new-found blessings of God's abundance!

I know you are grasping the truth of what I'm telling you. I am talking to you about breaking out of the old ruts, of moving into a new stratum, a new level of life. Right now, your most distant horizon of abundance forms the foundation for an entirely new life. God has something big for your life, but you must be willing to take it by force.

You must be willing to do battle and break out of your old concepts. You must be willing to fight the resistance you will feel from the devil and from your old insufficiency mentality. You will have to fight the "here-we-go-again" feeling that comes over you when your preacher calls for the offering, when you hear an appeal on a telethon, or receive the monthly ministry donor letter.

You must fight to achieve a new level of understanding, and realize that every offering is an opportunity to plant the seeds that will bring forth more fruit. In turn, you can plant even more seeds into *your ministry of giving!* Remember: whenever you give in an offering to meet the budget, you are also giving to help meet your own needs — now, and in the future.

You must fight the urge to give only five dollars when God is clearly telling you in your spirit to give fifty. You will make this breakthrough in your finances only through a violent overthrow of your old thinking and the forceful implanting of the mind of Christ into your giving.

You must continue to change the way you think. As you do, you will receive greater abundance in your life. Continue to violently react to the poverty in your life. It is time to break out of that struggle, and press toward the breakthrough. For years, I sat around passively hoping, waiting for something to happen. Nothing did. Finally, I had to decide to get violent, and by force, to break through.

If that is what is in your heart right now, you have made the decision to change your life. You've made up your mind that you are going to have a breakthrough, but you will have to become violent to get it.

The hard truth is that we do not have a chance of reaching this world with the Good News of Jesus, His love, His new kind of living, until many more of the saints of God literally revolutionize their thinking and violently possess, by force, what God has for us.

Say this statement out loud with me: "Yes, I can have abundance so I can sow it into the things of God and the lives of others."

Aren't you glad you are learning that God

wants you to be blessed and rich? Continue to seize your blessing, so you can operate the ever-increasing gift of *giving* even more strongly every day.

Section VIII:
First Things First!

Lesson 55:
What Is God's Order?

To understand and apply God's principles of biblical economics so you can have *an active, effective ministry of giving* to finance the end-time harvest, you must first establish God's proper spiritual order in your life.

God the Father should be first. There's no question about that.

> **Jesus said unto him, Thou shalt love the Lord thy God with all thy heart, and with all thy soul, and with all thy mind.**
>
> **This is the first and great commandment.**
> **Matthew 22:37,38**

That's conclusive. God should be first. There's probably not a single soul in all of Christianity who would disagree with that statement. I do not know of one doctrine, one church, one preacher, one teacher or one Christian philosopher who would argue this principle.

But, to make any *major breakthrough* in the spiritual area of finances, your spiritual priorities must be absolutely straight. *God must be first in every aspect of your life,* not just in your passive agreement, but in your daily *actions.*

He must come before money. If you spend three minutes a day praying and ten hours a day going after more money, then who (or what) is your god?

He must come before your own career. If you spend all of your waking hours concentrating on career moves, taking no time to ask God for His will, then who (or what) is your god?

He must come before your own pleasure. If all of your leisure time is spent pursuing pleasure, reading magazines and watching television, while the Bible gathers dust on the dining room table, then who (or what) is your god?

Yes, God must come even before your precious spouse or children. Family picnics and other family outings assume their proper priority only when God is the head of your household.

God is first!

> I am the Lord thy God, which have brought thee out of the land of Egypt, out of the house of bondage.
>
> Thou shalt have no other gods before me.
> Exodus 20:2,3

If you want to have an *active, effective ministry of giving,* you must prayerfully and carefully make sure that your priorities are clear and in scriptural order. If there is any area of your life that ranks above God, then repent of that wrong emphasis, and prayerfully put your heart in proper order.

Remember: Jesus Himself put this order into focus in the book of Matthew, Chapter 6, verse 33:

> But seek ye first the kingdom of God, and
> his righteousness; and all these things shall be
> added unto you.

This careful ordering of our priorities is the way
to bring forth the things we need.

Lesson 56:
God Is First; Who Is Second?

Like many people, you may get very upset
when you find out who should come after God in
your list of priorities — you.

That's right. The Bible declares that *you* are second:

> And the second (commandment) is like unto
> it, Thou shalt love thy neighbour as thyself.
>
> On these two commandments hang all the
> law and the prophets.
>
> Matthew 22:39,40

Most of us are pretty good about taking care of
ourselves. Each month we manage to make the house
payments, the car payments, and meet most of our
needs, including clothing, education and even entertainment. We know fairly well how to love ourselves
second, but the hard part is that we are supposed to
love our neighbor in the same way!

You and I are dedicated to meeting our own
needs, but the Word of God says that we need to be
dedicated to meeting the needs of the world as well.
Our "neighbor" is every man, woman, boy and girl in
the world, regardless of whether he or she is saved or
lost.

The Church understands clearly who to love
first: God. And, we love ourselves second. We man-

age to meet our own needs. But, if Jesus placed our fellow man in a position equal to our own, then to fulfill that commandment (the second most important commandment), you and I must be conscious of our neighbor's specific needs, whether they are spiritual, physical or financial.

To be in the center of God's will (and to avoid blocking any of the good things God has for you), you must have as much concern for the people in the world as you have for yourself. God wants *you* to prosper so you can help others around you to prosper spiritually, physically and financially!

If you get these two priorities straight, it won't be long before you will be in the center of God's will, and will begin to optimize the flow of God's abundance in your life. If all the saints caught this vision, it would be only a very short time until we would see the precious people of the world being drawn nearer to Jesus.

Third John 2 records John's wish, or prayer, for our prosperity and our health, but notice that both these benefits are linked to our soul's prosperity:

> **Beloved, I wish above all things that thou mayest prosper and be in health, even as thy soul prospereth.**

There is no prosperity for the soul which neglects the two greatest commandments. We must put God first, and ourselves and our neighbor second.

Remember, the soul which prospers brings material prosperity and health to its owner, but the soul which sins and rebels is bound for destruction:

The soul that sinneth, it shall die....
                                    Ezekiel 18:20

Lesson 57:
What About "the Church"?

Today, I want to ask you another question concerning priorities. Which comes first — your job, your family, or your place of worship?

Opinions differ.

Most Christians would probably pick their family. But if we can believe the Word, that is not the right answer.

When Isaac moved to Beersheba to live, the first thing he did was to *build an altar for worship:*

> And *he builded an altar there, and called upon the name of the Lord,* and pitched his tent there: and Isaac's servants digged a well.
>   **Genesis 26:25**

The second thing Isaac did was to *set up the place where his family would live:* he pitched his tent. Now, Isaac was a well digger, so the third thing he did was *supervise the digging of a well.*

Church.

Family.

Profession.

Isaac put his place of worship first, his family second, and his profession third.

In order to enjoy God's best, we must put God's priorities in order in our lives. The place where you receive your spiritual meat must have a top priority in your life. It may be your local church, a radio or television ministry, or a major literature ministry. Wherever you receive your spiritual nourishment, that place deserves a priority in your heart and in your finances.

Since you are now unleashing God's abundant blessings in your life through the *power* of giving, give top priority to your spiritual storehouse — the place where you receive your spiritual nourishment. Make out your tithe and offering check first, before you pay even a single bill. Set aside the firstfruits for your God.

Isaac put his place where he worshipped God first. You should follow that pattern in your life too.

Lesson 58:
Pay Bills or Tithe First?

To have an *active, effective ministry of giving* in your life, not only must your priorities concerning God be proper, but your priorities in your giving must be clear.

A major question many Christians ask as they begin to put their financial house in order is:

"Do I tithe before or after I pay my bills?"

Many people will pay all of their bills, and then, after all of their financial obligations are met, they will tithe to God out of the remaining money. That may be common practice, but it is not what the Bible teaches in Deuteronomy 26, verses 2, 5, 10 and 12:

> ...thou shalt take of *the first of all the fruit*
> **of the earth, which thou shalt bring of thy land**
> **that the Lord thy God giveth thee, and shalt put it**

in a basket, and shalt go unto the place which the Lord thy God shall choose to place his name there.

And thou shalt speak and say before the Lord thy God....

And now, behold, I have brought the *first-fruits* of the land, which thou, O Lord, hast given me. And thou shalt set it before the Lord thy God, and worship before the Lord thy God:....

When thou hast made an end of tithing....

The process of bringing the *firstfruits* to God (before paying the bills) is called tithing. God's Word says that you should tithe first, before you do anything else with your "fruits" (finances)!

Now, you may say, "But, Brother John, if I tithe first, I won't have enough to pay my bills."

Think how full of unbelief that statement is. If you believe that, then you are not believing that the tithe will open the windows of heaven to you.

You see, tithing establishes a new relationship between you and God. It brings you before the open windows of heaven. Literally, this means that the treasure house of God is now open to you. If you put God first, as He says to do, then surely He will bless you.

To break through into abounding finances, you must not listen to the devil on this matter; he would have you become fearful and pay your bills first. As sure as you do, more times than not, there will not be enough left over to tithe, much less to make an additional goodwill offering before God.

Please be wise enough to see that if you tithe and make offerings after all the bills are paid, you are leaving yourself at the mercy of your bills. With this action, your tithe and offerings are subject to and under the control of your bills.

But, if you tithe first, and give a generous offering, then your bills become subject and under the control of your tithes and offerings.

Remember: Malachi 3:10,11 speaks of open windows for tithing and uninterrupted harvests for your offerings. As long as you have bills, *always* keep them in their proper place behind the tithe. Put God's business first and foremost, and He will put your business first.

Lesson 59: What About Paying the Men of God Who Teach the Word?

The Bible instructs a teacher to teach the entire Word of God, no matter what the situation. In this lesson, I'm really trusting God that you will *hear His Word*. Tremendous future blessings depend upon on how you receive this lesson.

Think about the many men and women of God who spiritually bless your life. You have the pastor of your church, Bible teachers, evangelists, missionaries, television and radio ministers, and many, many more.

Read 1 Timothy 5:17 and 18:

> **Let the elders that rule well be counted worthy of double honour, especially they who labour in the word and doctrine.**

> **For the scripture saith, Thou shalt not muzzle the ox that treadeth out the corn. And, the labourer is worthy of his reward.**

The laborer (ordinary worker) is worthy of his hire, but those who labor in the Word are worthy of *double* pay.

Elijah understood this principle when he commanded the hungry widow of Zarephath to give her last bit of food to him, the man of God:

> ...but make me thereof a little cake *first,* and bring it unto me, and *after* make for thee and thy son.
>
> **1 Kings 17:13**

Elijah told the widow to make the cake for him first, not because he didn't care about her needs, but because he knew that as she provided for the servant of God, the Lord would provide for her and her family.

And He *did!*

> And she went and did according to the saying of Elijah: and she, and he, and her house, did eat many days.
>
> And the barrel of meal wasted not (was not used up), neither did the cruse of oil fail....
>
> **1 Kings 17:15,16**

The Bible teaches very clearly that the men of God who minister to you in your life need to receive high priority when you begin to distribute the dollars that you put into the Gospel.

> Let him that is taught in the word communicate unto (share with) him that teacheth in all good things.
>
> **Galatians 6:6**

Lesson 60: The Primary Truth — Giving Goes Before Receiving

You have been learning in the last few days that God sets priorities. In this lesson, I want to emphasize the most elementary priority of all. I almost left it unmentioned, but God said to most surely include it:

Giving always goes before receiving!

The world would have you believe that first you receive, and then you give. So many times I have heard good, honest, sincere Christians say:

"Oh, Brother John, when I receive a million dollars, I'm going to give a great amount to the work of the Lord! You just watch. I know I will."

Well, strangely, the Bible contradicts that bit of human reasoning. The Bible says that a person must be faithful in a little, or he will never have the opportunity to be faithful in a lot:

> **He that is faithful in that which is least is faithful also in much: and he that is unjust in the least is unjust also in much.**
>
> **Luke 16:10**

Now read this sentence carefully: Waiting for abundance before starting to give will not insure the giving of large gifts; it will actually insure just the opposite — you will not give at all.

First things come first. If you want to receive from God, you must first begin to give. The Bible clearly teaches this principle over and over again, throughout the entire book. Luke 6:38 says to give first, then it will be given to you. Malachi 3:10 says to tithe first, then God will open the windows of heaven, and pour out a blessing upon you.

Even unsaved farmers know this primary principle: You must sow before you can reap. You will *never* hear a farmer say:

"I'm not going to do any planting just yet. God must first give me a harvest of wheat, *then* I'll plant my seed in the field."

Every farmer knows that such a thing simply will not happen. He knows that he must first plant seeds, no matter how few he has, and then he will get back a harvest.

Does the Lord give you salvation first, and then you give your heart to Him? Of course not. First *you give* your heart to Him, and then *He gives* you eternal life.

God's principle of first planting, then reaping, is firmly entrenched in every aspect of life, from Genesis to Revelation, from farming to the propagation of every species.

There is no hope of increase without seeding!

Remember what Solomon said:

> To every thing there is a season, and a time to every purpose under the heaven:
>
> A time to be born, and a time to die; *a time to plant, and a time to pluck up that which is planted.*
>
> **Ecclesiastes 3:1,2**

First Things First!
In Summary

Only one time in the Bible do we read where someone inquired of Jesus how to be saved. The one who posed this question was a rich young ruler who asked: **...Good Master, what shall I do to inherit eternal life?** (Luke 18:18).

As amazing as it may seem, Jesus preached a money sermon to that young man. He told him to go sell all he had, and give it to the poor, and follow

Him! Why did Jesus do this? Do you think it was because He wanted that young fellow to be poor?

No! A thousand times no!

It was because Jesus wanted him to get his priorities straight! If the young ruler had agreed to give up his riches for the sake of the Gospel, Jesus would have surely given the riches back to him greatly increased. Scripture clearly teaches this principle as we have seen. Also, Scripture teaches that it is impossible to go broke giving to the poor.

> **He that hath pity upon the poor lendeth unto the Lord; and that which he hath given will he pay him again.**
>
> **Proverbs 19:17**

Now remember: God must be your first priority. When His priority is established over your money, then the Lord can begin to do some mighty things in your life and in your finances.

Set your priorities.

Deuteronomy 8:18 sets the priority for finances:

> **But thou shalt remember the Lord thy God: for it is he that giveth thee power to get wealth, *that he may establish his covenant....***

And what is the covenant?

> **And I will make of thee a great nation, and I will bless thee, and make thy name great; and *thou shalt be a blessing.***
>
> **Genesis 12:2**

Yes, God wants to bless you, so you can go forth and fulfill His *second priority:* to love and bless your neighbor as you are loved and blessed yourself. God has given you and me the power to get wealth so that we (the whole Body of Christ) can go forth and preach the Gospel throughout the entire world without apologizing to anyone, without fussing and fighting over past-due bills, and without large extentions of credit.

Yes, God has given us the power to get wealth so we can bring the Gospel to the world, without going into debt.

Set your priorities.

Go boldly beyond being blessed into being a blessing. You cannot be a blessing to others until you personally have been blessed by God. Surely, now is the time for the Church to violently break out of the poverty cycle. It is time to stop the trickle of financial blessings in our lives, and make some violent breakthroughs that will properly fund our end-time vision of reaching the world with the Word of God.

Remember, along with a knowledge of God's plan for abundance, it takes decisive action.

The farmer must first plant seeds. Sometimes he sows in very hard ground, from early morning to late at night, in the hot sun, often without lunch. If he wants a great harvest, he must fight to get seed into the ground.

The same is true in your financial walk. Sometimes seed planting is very hard. Circumstances may say, "You cannot afford to give fifty dollars."

But do it anyway.

Circumstances may say, "You cannot afford to tithe before you pay your bills."

But do it anyway.

Circumstances may say, "You cannot afford to give a specific love gift to your pastor *and* the offering God has instructed for you to send to some special ministry."

But do it anyway.

Breakthroughs in sowing (giving) always go before breakthroughs in harvesting (receiving).

Remember Galatians 6:9:

> **And let us not be weary in well doing: for in due season we shall reap (receive), if we faint not.**

Section IX:
God's Gift-Giving Example

Lesson 61:
The Gift of Salvation

If we are to become proper givers, then our giving must be patterned after the greatest gift-giver of all — God, our heavenly Father. He freely gave us the greatest of all gifts — salvation:

> For by grace are ye saved through faith; and that not of yourselves: it is *the gift of God:*
>
> Not of works, lest any man should boast.
> Ephesians 2:8,9

God gives us *salvation*, through faith, as a free gift! No one can "earn" his salvation through good works; it is a miracle gift from God. When God sent Jesus Christ to this earth, Jesus was a free gift, sent to provide us with salvation and eternal life.

> O wretched man that I am! who shall deliver me from the body of this death?
>
> I thank God through Jesus Christ our Lord....
> Romans 7:24,25

> For God so loved the world, that *He gave* His only begotten Son, that whoever believes in Him should not perish but have everlasting life.
>
> For God did not send His Son into the

world to condemn the world, but that the world
through Him might be saved.

John 3:16,17 NKJ

The only thing anyone can do to receive God's
free gift of salvation is to simply tell the Lord, "Yes,
Father, I do accept Jesus into my heart as the Lord
and Savior of my life."

Do you see how totally free the gift of salvation
is? Eternal life can only be *accepted* as a gift; there is
absolutely nothing anyone can do in his own strength
to ever earn it!

Always remember this principle whenever you
give. Realize that the recipient of your gift may have
partially "earned" the gift by good conduct, by some
work he or she did for you, by some ministry which
blessed you, or by providing you a donor gift in
recognition of your support. There is nothing wrong
with this, but remember that the motivation for this
kind of giving (while the giving itself is scriptural) is
not of the same quality of motivation as the gift of
your salvation.

I recommend that you include not only those
who have blessed you in your giving, but some who
have done absolutely nothing to earn or deserve your
gift: the poor, the hungry, a ministry that doesn't even
know you are alive. Just send that person or group an
offering because you know God wants you to.

Lesson 62:
Faith

In the last lesson, we learned that God freely
saves us:

> **For by grace are ye saved through faith; and that not of yourselves: it is the gift of God:**
>
> **Not of works, lest any man should boast.**
>
> **Ephesians 2:8,9**

Salvation comes as a gift through faith, and our faith is a free gift, too (Rom. 12:3). Faith is a critical part of our walk with God:

> **But without faith it is *impossible to please him:* for he that cometh to God must believe that he is, and that he is a rewarder of them that diligently seek him.**
>
> **Hebrews 11:6**

But where does our faith come from?

> **Looking unto Jesus the *author* and finisher *of our faith;* who for the joy that was set before him endured the cross, despising the shame, and is set down at the right hand of the throne of God.**
>
> **Hebrews 12:2**

God freely gave us Jesus Christ and eternal salvation. And then, so we can please God and defeat the enemy in our day-to-day battles with our various circumstances, He freely *gave us faith.* This faith God gives us is vital if you and I are to break out of the bonds of insufficiency in which so many Christians languish this very day. This *God-given faith* is a major key to financial freedom.

Faith is a major ingredient in attaining the inheritance God has for you and me. The writer of Hebrews exhorts us:

> **That ye be not slothful, but followers of them who through faith and patience inherit the promises.**
>
> **Hebrews 6:12**

The promises of God (the abundant supply) are greatly dependent upon faith. Guard your faith. Thank God for it, and give it plenty of exercise. As you give, believe in faith that you will receive more and more so you can give away more and more fruit from your harvest:

> For God, who gives seed to the farmer to plant, and later on, good crops to harvest and eat, will give you more and more seed to plant and will make it grow so that you can give away more and more fruit from your harvest.
>
> Yes, God will give you much so that you can give away much....

> **2 Corinthians 9:10,11 TLB**

Lesson 63:
The Gift of the Holy Spirit

God has promised that when the Holy Spirit enters your life, several marvelous things will happen:

1. God also freely bestows upon you the fruit of the Spirit:

> But the fruit of the Spirit is love, joy, peace, longsuffering, gentleness, goodness, faith,
>
> Meekness, temperance: against such there is no law.

> **Galatians 5:22,23**

2. You will receive *power* and be a *witness:*

> ...ye shall receive power, after that the Holy Ghost is come upon you: and ye shall be witnesses unto me both in Jerusalem, and in all Judaea, and in Samaria, and unto the uttermost part of the earth.

> **Acts 1:8**

3. Through the indwelling Holy Spirit, and the

wonderful prayer language He gives you, you will be
able to build up the faith God has given you.*

> **But ye, beloved, building up yourselves on
> your most holy faith, praying in the Holy Ghost.**
>
> **Jude 20**

4. The Holy Spirit will help you pray in accordance with God's will:

> **Likewise the Spirit also helpeth our infir-
> mities: for we know not what we should pray for
> as we ought: but the Spirit itself maketh interces-
> sion for us with groanings which cannot be
> uttered.**
>
> **Romans 8:26**

Now, here's the true miracle of the Holy Spirit:
God gives His Holy Spirit to us freely. *All we have to
do to receive is ask!*

> **If ye then, being evil, know how to give
> good gifts unto your children: how much more
> shall your heavenly Father give the Holy Spirit to
> them that ask him?**
>
> **Luke 11:13**

Are you beginning to grasp what a grand giver
God is? He freely gives us all the things we need to
live well in this life, and also in eternity!

This series of lessons on giving is not taking
you away from God, but is bringing you more into
His likeness and image:

> **While we look not at the things which are
> seen, but at the things which are not seen: for the**

---

*Remember that faith comes by hearing the Word of God according to Romans 10:17.
You must study God's Word to obtain faith and use your prayer language to build up
yourself on your faith.

things which are seen are temporal; but the things which are not seen are eternal.

2 Corinthians 4:18

I believe now, at the close of Lesson 63, you are reaching the point of breakthrough. If we are sons of God, then we should show His personality to the world. God is the greatest of all givers, and we must be like Him — *great givers*.

Lesson 64:
God Gives Freely and Joyfully!

Our great, giving God is continuously giving to us all things that pertain to life and godliness:

According as his divine power hath given unto us *all things that pertain unto life and godliness*, through the knowledge of him that hath called us to glory and virtue.

2 Peter 1:3

Many things pertain unto life. Just think of all the things this encompasses. Gasoline for our cars is something pertaining to life. Although it seems that the price of gasoline is only going up, God knows that we need fuel, and the Bible guarantees that our God will supply "all things that pertain unto life," including groceries, clothes, housing and a job. No matter how high the price of groceries, clothes or gasoline goes, it does not matter. Our God promises to supply every need in our lives.

By now this simple truth must be sinking into your spirit. God wants to bless us so wonderfully, so completely, so powerfully, because He wants us to become great givers — *like Him!* God wants you and me to abundantly receive so we can abundantly give.

He wants to position us for the greater blessings He will bring upon us, for He said it is more blessed to give than to receive.

As you learn to give in your everyday life, you are unleashing the process that will make you more like God. He is the greatest giver, and He wants you to become like Him:

> Herein is our love made perfect, that we may have boldness in the day of judgment: because as *he is, so are we in this world.*
>
> 1 John 4:17

God sees us as He is — and so we are, in this world. Can you lay hold of that thought and grasp its eternal significance?

God sees us as He is, in this world, manifesting a walking, talking, proof-producing ministry that brings forth a duplication of Christ on the earth. Isn't it wonderful to know that, through your giving, soon your prosperity will grow to the point that you will be able to bless all men you meet?

Truly, you are on the threshold of moving beyond receiving the blessing into actually *becoming a blessing.*

> All scripture is given by inspiration of God, and is profitable for doctrine, for reproof, for correction, for instruction in righteousness:
>
> That the man of God may be perfect, thoroughly furnished unto all good works.
>
> 2 Timothy 3:16,17

Lesson 65: Jesus Is a Great Giver

When God's first Son, Jesus Christ, took on the whole nature and personality of His heavenly Father,

He, too, was a great giver. Hear what the Word says about Jesus:

> **Wherefore he saith, When he ascended up on high, he led captivity captive, and *gave gifts unto men.***
>
> **Ephesians 4:8**

Aren't you glad that the precious recorded words of Jesus are faithfully preserved by the Holy Spirit? They so clearly reveal why He personally came down to this earth. Hear Him as He speaks to those who heard these words many years ago:

> *...I am come that they might have life, and that they might have it (new life) more abundantly.*
>
> **John 10:10**

"I am come that they might have...."

Jesus did not come down to earth to make us give up good things and lead a life of sorrow, poverty and depression. If you carefully read the words of the Bible, you will find that the true intention of God was not to remove us from the world and its goods, but to actually have us take over this world and its goods.

> **Beloved, I wish above all things that thou mayest prosper and be in health, even as thy soul prospereth.**
>
> **3 John 2**

If we are going to function as Jesus functioned, we must be concerned about more than just our own abundance. We must also be concerned about our brothers and sisters around the world. We must care whether they have all that they need. This is not our choice, it is a command:

> *Give to him that asketh thee,* **and from him that would borrow of thee turn not thou away.**
>
> **Matthew 5:42**

How will we do this if we are broke and in want ourselves? How can we give to everyone who asks of us? Jesus did. He knew that His heavenly Father would supply everything He needed. He came to give; He literally tapped into the unlimited supply. And He tells us to walk in the same footsteps, doing the same things He did:

> **Heal the sick, cleanse the lepers, raise the dead, cast out devils:** *freely ye have received, freely give.*
>
> **Matthew 10:8**

In freely giving, we open the storehouses of God, and we unleash an unending supply.

Jesus wants you and me to alleviate misery, pain and sorrow — to overcome death, disease and sickness all over the world! Jesus wants us to generously give out of His unending supply of health and power. He wants our giving to go beyond salvation, health and deliverance. He wants us to give alms to the poor, water to the thirsty, the bread of life to those in need. The Scriptures which deal with these benevolent gifts are too numerous to mention.

I know that with each lesson in this last third of our study, you are growing more confident that your decision to imitate Jesus in the grace of giving is one of the best you have ever made.

Many times this new grace doesn't even require financial resources. You can give peace to the depressed, joy to the unhappy, salvation to the lost, confidence to the inhibited. Yes, you are even now leaving the realm of just the intangible and are becoming a giver of the tangible.

Even if you haven't given $10,000 yet, you are changing your lifestyle from that of a consumer to that of a provider. You are literally beginning to come forth in a measure of the stature of Christ. Say this out loud now:

"My Lord Jesus came that men might have life more abundantly, and as His servant, I am now here that men might have life more abundantly."

Lesson 66:
The Holy Spirit Is a Great Giver

We have seen that God is a great giver and that Jesus is a great giver. So, it must spiritually follow that the Holy Spirit is also a great giver.

The Word of God clearly shows that this is so. Every informed Christian knows that when you submit yourself to the Holy Spirit, He immediately becomes an abundant source of priceless treasures. With the Holy Spirit in us, we have the fruit of the Spirit available to us:

But the fruit of the Spirit is love, joy, peace, longsuffering, gentleness, goodness, faith,

Meekness, temperance....

Galatians 5:22,23

We also have the gifts of the Spirit available to us: wisdom, knowledge, faith, healing, miracles, prophecy, the ability to distinguish between spirits, different kinds of tongues, interpretation of tongues.

All of these gifts are documented in First Corinthians 12:1-11. The treasure chest of the Holy Spirit is not understandable by sense knowledge, the depth of the riches of God must be grasped through spiritual perception:

> ...Eye hath not seen, nor ear heard, neither have entered into the heart of man, the things which God hath prepared for them that love him.
>
> But God hath revealed them unto us by his Spirit....
>
> 1 Corinthians 2:9,10

And there's still more. The very *power to witness* is a free gift of the Holy Spirit:

> And when they had prayed, the place where they were assembled together was shaken; and they were all filled with the Holy Spirit, and *they spoke the word of God with boldness.*
>
> Acts 4:31 NKJ

Are you beginning to see how much God has in store for us in His everlasting, abundant, inexhaustible storehouse? He has so much for you and me that there is literally no place on earth which can contain all of the physical and spiritual blessings of God the Father, Jesus the Son, and the Holy Spirit.

Remember: the things that the Holy Spirit has for us are infinitely more valuable than all worldly treasures. If we neglect them and seek after material treasures alone, we will do eternal damage to ourselves.

Simon, the sorcerer, whose story is found in Acts 8:14-24, tried to put a money value on the gifts of the Holy Ghost. He was cursed, and his money with him, because he lacked a full understanding of the superior value of the Spirit's gifts.

It is fine to attain earthly treasure, but we must pursue above all else the gifts of the Spirit, for they are eternal.

Lesson 67: A Gift Will Always Prosper the Giver

Now that you have refreshed and renewed your mind with the knowledge of our great God's spirit of giving, you can more easily understand that the world's ways are not God's ways. Surely, the biblical principles in this section have amplified that point.

By the world's principles of economics, when you give something away, you then have less. If you give away money or land or food, that leaves you with less of the thing you have given away.

But such is not the case according to God's principles of economics. He teaches that when you give something away, it *always* ends up returning to you, *multiplied*.

In God's economy, any gift you give away always ends up prospering you beyond where you were when you gave the gift in the first place. Simply stated, you cannot lose ground by giving to God.

According to God's principles of economics, when you give a gift, you release His energy into your own life to duplicate the gift in multiplied quantity. Gifts become very powerful forces that reach beyond the natural realm into the spirit realm and increase themselves, some thirtyfold, some sixtyfold, and some a hundredfold.

When you give something to someone, even if what you give is thrown away, it doesn't stop the spiritual energy of that gift from working towards *prospering your life*. Even if it is misused, that gift will begin to prosper you.

Notice, God says that He will prosper the giver, not the gift.

The world says that giving a gift depletes wealth. *Logic says* that when a person gives something away, he no longer has it. But, *God's Word says* that a gift does not deplete a person's assets, it *increases* them!

Because of the principles taught in God's Word, every gift you give becomes an invisible miracle force that draws right back to you more of whatever you have given away. That is a powerful concept.

Look now at another marvelous promise God makes to the giver.

> **Many will entreat the favor of the prince:**
> and *every man is a friend to him that giveth gifts.*
> **Proverbs 19:6**

When you give gifts, it shows that you are willing to meet the needs of others. The Bible teaches that because of your generous nature, you will have friends, your gift will not "buy" their friendship, but your heart, your generous nature, will supernaturally attract people with your well-being at heart. The dimension of this supernatural power of God that is released by the God-motivated giver even reaches into the camp of the person's enemies. When we obey God in every aspect of our lives, which includes giving as He directs us, even our enemies are caught up in a new attitude toward us:

> **When a man's ways please the Lord, he maketh even his enemies to be at peace with him.**
>
> **Proverbs 16:7**

Your gift is a natural key that unleashes a supernatural miracle-working force in your life. You may say: "Well, Brother John, I just don't believe that."

Friend, it does not make any difference whether you believe it or not. The Bible says it, and it's a fact. God wants you to have friends, and He promises friends as one of the rewards for being a gracious *giver*.

Lesson 68: God's Giving Guarantee

We have seen that giving is a gift of God. It is "God-like" and conforms us closer to His image. We learned that giving makes a person prosperous, and that it releases supernatural miracle-working power in and through his life.

Now, I want you to realize that this entire process is completely guaranteed! It is a spiritual law, as powerful and as dependable as any natural law:

> **Give, and it shall be given unto you; good measure, pressed down, and shaken together, and running over, shall men give into your bosom. For with the same measure that ye mete withal (measure), it shall be measured to you again.**
>
> **Luke 6:38**

> **Be not deceived; God is not mocked: for whatsoever a man soweth, that shall he also reap.**
>
> **Galatians 6:7**

So often, when the offering plate is passed in

church, or a ministry asks for your support, a question goes through your mind: "I wonder if I can afford to give?"

Well, you are asking the wrong question. The question you should be asking yourself is: "Can I afford *not* to give?"

You see, God has guaranteed that a gift always comes back, in good measure, pressed down, shaken together, and running over. Whatever you sow you will reap.

That is certainly better than Wall Street can promise you! That's better than the interest at your local savings and loan! The Bible says that men will give into your bosom (notice, it does not just say the saints will give to you, it simply says "men"). Today, there are more than 4.8 billion people in the world — that's how many instruments God has available to bless you.

That's God's promise. When you give to His work, you can trust God to give back to you.

Once again, this process of returning the gift to you is not just left to chance. It is a guaranteed rate of return: *it comes back to you in the same measure that you gave*. If you give a thimbleful, you will get back many times that amount of blessing. If you give a teaspoonful, you will get back many times that amount of blessing. But, if you upgrade your gift and start giving by the shovelful, look out, because God must move up to shovels of blessings.

Do not be afraid if you want to move into the "big league" of giving. God has truckloads for those who give by the truckload. You see, He promises the same measure as is given. Give a little, and you will receive a little. Give a lot, and God will overwhelm you with His blessings in return.

> But remember this — if you give little, you will get little. A farmer who plants just a few seeds will get only a small crop, but if he plants much, he will reap much.
>
> **2 Corinthians 9:6 TLB**

Lesson 69: You Can Afford a Gift

You believed God for your salvation — and got it.

You believed God for your healing — and got it.

You believed God when you asked for the Holy Spirit — and got Him.

Now, surely, you can believe God in gift-giving. When you do, I believe you will see something similar to the time of Moses when the giving was so generous that Moses actually commanded:

> ...Let neither man nor woman make any more work for the offering of the sanctuary. So the people were restrained from bringing.
>
> For the stuff they had was *sufficient for all the work to make it, and too much.*
>
> **Exodus 36:6,7**

Every mission outreach could have more than enough. Every Christian television program could have more than enough. Every church expansion program, every Sunday school auditorium, every Christian camp, could have more than enough. Every home in the world could have a Christian worker knocking at the door, inviting the family members to become children of God, and offering to meet their needs, no matter what they are.

What a miracle day that would be! But for it to happen, we who are being enlightened to the principles of biblical economics must press into dimensions of giving and receiving that will release such a flood-tide of abundance into the Gospel ministry that Satan's lie of insufficiency will be rendered powerless. As our brethren lay hold upon this truth in mass numbers, they can eradicate hunger, want, and insufficiency from our planet.

Our giving can usher in a new day of plenty in a new Kingdom of God here on earth.

All of Israel was involved in giving. That's why Moses had to command the people to stop. There simply was too much. Call us dreamers, if you must, but the truth of God in regard to abundance will come to pass. *The reapers will overtake the sowers.*

Lesson 70: There's More Than Enough

God is building a Church to be His special dwelling place in these last days. There is a world out there to reach, and God wants to reach it. But, if you and I are continuously sitting around trying to figure out how much we want to give, we will probably talk ourselves out of 90 percent of what God wants us to give *so He can really bless us!*

Hold this truth in your spirit. Our King of Kings, our Lord of Lords, is *not low on funds!* He isn't about to go bankrupt. But He is trying to keep us from getting low on funds or going bankrupt. He has devised this wonderful plan for replenishing our treasury and instructs us in the supernatural realm of creating what we need.

Yes, miracle power awaits you if you dare to apply God's method of obtaining. You know how God obtains; He does it by giving:

> **For God so loved the world, that *he gave* his only begotten Son, that whosoever believeth in him should not perish, but have everlasting life.**
>
> **John 3:16**

When God wanted sons, He gave His Son; now He has millions of sons.

This principle worked for the widow of Zarephath. There was more than enough for her when *she gave* to the prophet Elijah.

There was more than enough for Moses when he called upon his people to bring offerings to the sanctuary.

There was more than enough when Jesus had to feed the multitudes with five loaves and two fishes.

And there is more than enough for your life!

Do you honestly believe that you could give more to God than God could give back to you? Can you really imagine God watching you give, and then saying, "Oops, that did it. You just gave me more than My current supply of blessings. There's no possible way I can ever give *that much* back to you." Do you really think that you could ever break the bank of heaven?

Absolutely not. It will never happen.

Remember: we read that Moses had "too much" because the saints of God in his day grasped this spiritual concept. Well, just read one bit of the description concerning the sanctuary they were building:

> **And he overlaid the boards with gold, and made their rings of gold to be places for the bars, and overlaid the bars with gold.**
>
> **Exodus 36:34**

Notice that when the abundance of God is envisioned and acted upon there is no need for scrimping.

Realize it; visualize it; verbalize it. There is more than enough for you!

God's Gift-Giving Example In Summary

All well-informed Christians understand that they are made in the *image and likeness* of God. However, sometimes we fail to grasp exactly what that image and likeness is.

God is a giver; *Jesus Christ* is a giver; *the Holy Spirit* is a giver. If you are to live in the measure of the image and likeness of God, you must become *a great giver.*

You may be currently giving tiny eyedropper-sized gifts; God desires more for your life. Eyedropper-sized blessings will not sustain you in these end-times.

You need to go beyond giving the minimum to giving the maximum. To get that kind of a breakthrough, you will have to become violent.

When you were first saved, you strongly and aggressively defeated the forces of evil which came against you. You were told by your neighbors, friends, and sometimes even family members, that you were not the way you used to be.

Praise God!

If you had continued in a passive posture, you would never have received your salvation break-through; you would have undoubtedly gone back to your old life. You remember how you had to bring forth a violent defense in the spirit world to win the victory over the devil.

When you first heard about healing, you had to abandon your false beliefs that healing is not for our day. It took strong faith to lay hands on someone the first time and pray for his or her healing. You did not want to do it. It was not comfortable. But you went ahead, and violently pressed back the negative forces — and God brought the healing.

The first time you heard about the Holy Spirit and opened yourself up to speaking in new tongues, it felt awkward. No passive effort would have taken you into that *breakthrough* of receiving the Holy Spirit. You had to violently break away from your misconceptions and open your mouth and speak forth those wonderful new utterances that were forming in your mind.

And now, today, you are in the process of another major *spiritual breakthrough* — a fantastic, supernatural financial breakthrough. Even now it is stirring in the heavenly realm around you. But, it will not come to full manifestation without a violent, forceful effort on your part.

The next time the offering basket comes to you in church, Satan will try to rob you of the break-through victory.

"You can't afford to give," he will try to tell you. "You have already given quite a bit." This is not your subconscious mind talking. It is the enemy. He wants to rob you and see you destitute.

Violently attack him by saying: "Get behind me, Satan. Get out of this matter. It is none of your business. All of my substance, my money, my equity, and my potential income, is already dedicated to Jesus Christ, my Lord and Savior. I dedicated it to Him, and it will be used to spread the Gospel around the world as He leads me to give. And, now I stand on *God's promise* that He will return to me everything I give to Him — in even greater proportion than I gave — so I can give even more next time!"

When the offering basket comes to you, don't just throw your money in. Take time to pray over your money, dedicate it to the Lord, and put it into the basket with confidence, knowing that the return is guaranteed by God. The simple act of putting your money in the basket is a spiritual step which releases God's miracle-working power into your financial life.

There are three steps you should take when giving your money to God:

1. *Decide* (how much God is saying to give).

2. *Dedicate* (set the money apart as holy money, dedicated to God).

3. *Deposit* (release the money at your earliest convenience).

You are now well into the financial breakthrough you have desired for so long! Always remember to give a bit beyond your comfort zone. Don't ever give only what you can afford. Remember: you are not sacrificially giving out of your great need, you are literally giving your way to financial prosperity.

Take the devil "to the woodshed" with your next offering! Put him in his place under your feet by your giving.

Even now the abundance of God is moving upon you:

> **And all these blessings shall come on thee, and overtake thee, if thou shalt hearken unto the voice of the Lord thy God.**
>
> **Deuteronomy 28:2**

Section X:
Five Kinds of Giving

Lesson 71:
The Tithe...Is It Still Necessary?

There is probably more confusion in the Body of Christ about tithing than any other single type of giving. But God is not the author of confusion, and His Word on the tithe is clear:

> *Will a man rob God? Yet ye have robbed me. But ye say, Wherein have we robbed thee? In tithes and offerings.*
>
> Ye are cursed with a curse: for ye have robbed me, even this whole nation.
>
> Bring ye all the tithes into the storehouse, that there may be meat (food) in mine house, and prove me now herewith, saith the Lord of hosts, if I will not open (for) you the windows of heaven, and pour you out a blessing, that there shall not be room enough to receive it.
>
> Malachi 3:8-10

If you are going to receive the optimum God-kind of prosperity in your life, you must not overlook or underemphasize the basic building blocks of your biblical prosperity plan. It is an absolute necessity that you follow the biblical plan in the area of tithing. To get the windows of heaven open — and keep them open — you must tithe. *Tithing is not a biblical option.* The tithe is something you literally owe to God.

"Well, Brother John, that sure takes the spirituality out of giving," you may say. "You make it sound as if *tithing is an obligation,* and *not a free act of the will.*"

Please remember, these are not my thoughts. God says that if we do not tithe, we are committing robbery. He says we owe Him the tithe. There is one important distinction. The tithe is given, not at our discretion, but *because God commands it.* By faithfully bringing forth the tithe to Him, we establish our basic honesty and obedience. (Read Lev. 27:30-33, which clearly shows that the tithe belongs to the Lord.)

However, our offerings are given out of our own generosity. They are totally at our own discretion, and they establish the level of our concern for the things of God:

> **Every one must make up his own mind as to how much he should give. Don't force anyone to give more than he really wants to, for cheerful givers are the ones God prizes. God is able to make it up to you by giving you everything you need and more, so that there will not only be enough for your own needs, but plenty left over to give joyfully to others.**
>
> **2 Corinthians 9:7,8 TLB**

Remember: you and I are not being generous when we tithe. We are simply obeying God. For the Christian, *tithing is not an option.*

In Hebrews 7:1-10, we see that Abraham paid tithes. He paid them for himself, before the dispensation of the law, and also paid them for Levi, who lived under the dispensation of the law. In fact, Abraham tithed for all posterity — for his natural children (seed), and for the spiritual children (seed) who now live in the dispensation of grace:

> **And if ye be Christ's, then are ye Abraham's seed, and heirs according to the promise.**
>
> **Galatians 3:29**

The obligation of tithing reaches across the pre-law dispensations, the dispensation of the law, and now, into the post-law dispensation of grace.

Remember: the windows of heaven are opened by the faithful giving of tithes, making this basic giving (the tithe) absolutely necessary. For, without the windows of heaven open, nothing can flow from God to you or me.

Lesson 72:
Where Should the Tithe Be Given?

There is great controversy as to where the tithe should be given. Some say it should go to the local church. Others say Bible colleges should receive it. Still others want the tithe to go strictly for world evangelism.

What I understand to be the biblical answer is found in the third chapter of Malachi. There we see that the tithe goes into *"the storehouse."* The context indicates that this storehouse is the place where the "meat" (the Word of God) is kept and supplied to the saints:

> **Bring ye all the tithes into the storehouse, that there may be meat in mine house, and prove me now herewith, saith the Lord of hosts, if I will not open you the windows of heaven, and pour you out a blessing, that there shall not be room enough to receive it.**
>
> **Malachi 3:10**

189

Where are you being fed the unadulterated Word of God? This is the question you must answer to determine where to give your tithe. The place you are being spiritually fed should be your local church, and above every other place, that is where you should tithe.

But, the truth of the matter is that there are not enough local churches truly reaching into every level of society to make this a hard and fast rule for tithing. Many saints are sick or otherwise unable to journey to church. Perhaps some of these saints receive their spiritual "meat" from a Christian television or radio program, or a good ministry to shut-ins. Surely this is an exception to the general rule that the tithe should go to the local church.

Now, some local pastors may not agree with this, but I must be faithful to the convictions God gives me from His Word. I trust that the teaching of my convictions about tithing will not cause a division between us. I understand the necessity for the tithe to go into a good local church, because for over twenty-five years I served as pastor of local churches, and I instructed my congregations that if they were receiving their spiritual meat from the church storehouse, that is where their tithe should go.

I never in all of my pastorate had any trouble with any reasonable saint of God failing to tithe. I found that the best way to insure that the tithe would come to our church was to be sure that our church was always full of good strong meat (the rightly divided Word of God).

Notice another aspect of this verse. God says to tithe, and "prove me." God is literally challenging you and me to put Him to the test in this matter of tithing. He wants the windows of heaven to be open in our lives. There is no other place in Scripture that I know of where God so clearly challenges us to test Him and His Word.

It must be becoming wonderfully clear that *God wants only to bless us!* But, He cannot do it through closed windows.

Let's keep up our momentum. We know we must tithe, and why, and now, according to the Word of God, we know where we should tithe. So, let's keep putting God to the test by consistently tithing, and we will see the windows of heaven open in our lives.

Remember: the tithe goes to the place where we receive our spiritual meat on a consistent basis. For most of us, it is our Full-Gospel church. If, however, you are in a church that does not preach the entire Word of God, go before God and prayerfully ask Him to lead you to a church near you that will systematically and faithfully feed you the meat of God's Word.

Lesson 73:
Can There Be Prosperity
Without the Tithe?

God wants to build an end-time temple — a holy habitation of God, not made with hands — but to do this He must have a great, end-time army of very special saints to accomplish His vision. That's not just a fancy idea, but it came to me by revelation after years and years of studying the Holy Bible. It's totally based upon Scripture.

God will give the responsibility of building this great end-time dwelling place to those who have been proven faithful in financial matters.

When King Josiah commissioned workers for the restoration of the temple, he gave the work to those craftsmen who had already proven themselves *faithful* in their *financial transactions:*

> **And let them deliver it into the hand of the doers of the work...to repair the breaches of the house,**

> **Unto carpenters, and builders, and masons, and to buy timber and hewn stone to repair the house,**

> **Howbeit** *there was no reckoning made with them of the money that was delivered into their hand, because they dealt faithfully.*
>
> 2 Kings 22:5-7

These men were not chosen to partake in this labor because they had *promised* to be faithful, they were chosen because they had already *proven* themselves to be faithful! When it came time for King Josiah to choose who would work in the great restoration of the temple, God told the king to select these men because they had an established record of *dealing faithfully in their finances.*

God uses people who are faithful in their finances, and tithing is part of that faithfulness.

Throughout the world many people have said to me, "Oh, Brother John, when I get a large sum of money (such as an inheritance, or sweepstakes winnings, or a windfall from some get-rich-quick scheme), then I will become a faithful giver of tithes to the Lord."

That is not God's way!

First, God *requires* that we be faithful in the little matters, right where we are, in the midst of our present circumstances; then, afterwards, God will grant us an abundance.

That was true in the Old and New Testaments, and it is true today. In the parable of the talents, what did the ruler say to his faithful servant?

> His lord said unto him, Well done, good and faithful servant; *thou hast been faithful over a few things, I will make thee ruler over many things:* enter thou into the joy of thy lord.
>
> **Matthew 25:23**

And what did Jesus say to His disciples about faithfulness?

> He that is faithful in that which is least is faithful also in much: and he that is unjust in the least is unjust also in much.
>
> **Luke 16:10**

If you want to be a part of the next big move of God, don't just get your finances in order temporarily. Keep them in order from now on.

> Moreover it is required (not just desired) in stewards, that a man be found faithful.
>
> **1 Corinthians 4:2**

Lesson 74: What Is an Offering?

I am sure by now that you have realized an offering is greatly different from a tithe. The tithe is clearly ten percent of what has been earned, an amount set by God which is paid to Him as a debt, or as a non-negotiable obligation owed to Him. Failure to pay the tithe is plainly called robbery in God's Word.

I know that is frank and to the point, but there is no sense in beating around the bush with the Word of God. He says it, so what can we do other than just believe it and abandon all debate?

But an offering — now that's a different matter!

An offering is not a specified amount; it is totally discretionary on our part, an amount we freely give to God to establish a rate of return from Him that is *acceptable* or *desirable* to us. By the amount of our offering the measure, or rate, by which God will bless us and increase our substance is established:

> **...For with the same measure that ye mete withal (measure) it shall be measured to you again.**
> **Luke 6:38**

An offering is anything we give over and above our tithe. You and I are not generous givers in the eyes of God when we tithe — the tithe is simply evidence of honesty. It is simply paying God what we "owe" Him.

But, when we hear the voice of God leading us to help finance a struggling ministry in the Philippines, or a ministry fighting drug abuse in a certain city, now that is an offering — a *freewill love offering to our God!*

Who is going to tithe to a Christian home for abused children? The only people receiving "meat" from this "spiritual storehouse" would be the little abused children in the home — and they do not have the finances to support the institution. So that work, and many more projects in God's Kingdom, survive solely through the freewill offerings of God's prosperous people!

Remember: the principles of biblical economics only start when we tithe. They are set in motion when we give generous offerings. There is a great blessing in offerings, because our offering determines the measure God uses to give back to us. And, offerings are always a blessing to the ministries receiving them, since in many cases these offerings are God's way of meeting their needs.

Through our tithes and offerings, you and I will move into a dynamic new realm as mature Christians, working with God, ministering to the needs of a hurting and needy world:

> **And they went forth, and preached every where, the Lord working with them, and confirming the word with signs following. Amen.**
>
> **Mark 16:20**

Lesson 75: The Hidden Blessing of Giving to World Missions

When you seriously search God's Word, you discover there is a spiritual gift of giving. That spiritual gift has many different manifestations. One is the releasing of the tithe. Another is the giving of an offering. In this lesson, we will talk about a third type of giving: specific giving to world missions.

There is a *very special type of blessing* God gives to those who support world missions. Read this key verse in its context:

> **Now ye Philippians know also, that in the beginning of the gospel, when I departed from Macedonia** (on a great mission journey), **no church communicated** (shared) **with me as concerning giving and receiving, but ye only,**
>
> **For even in Thessalonica** (one of the mission fields) **ye sent once and again unto my necessity.**
>
> **Not because I desire a gift: but I desire fruit that may abound to your account....**
>
> *But my God shall supply all your need according to his riches in glory by Christ Jesus.*
>
> **Philippians 4:15-17,19**

The last verse of this scripture is continuously quoted out of context by well-meaning but uninformed Christians everywhere. They claim Philippians 4:19 because it sounds desirable. But read the entire passage in its God-given context. This promise is given to a very exclusive group — those who faithfully support world missions.

The context here shows that God will supply all the needs of those who are doing what the Philippians were doing — giving to world missions. But notice that God did not say He would supply their needs *out of* His riches in glory, but He clearly states that He will supply their needs *according* to His riches in glory.

Now, let him who has an ear hear what the Spirit of God is saying. This may not make sense to some of my readers, but it will witness to you if you are catching a vision of the mind of God. The promise reads, **"But my God shall supply all your need according to his riches in glory."** The word *according* speaks of God's blessing in the same *quality, not quantity,* as His own riches in glory!

God provides a way for you and me to have both abundance and quality. Don't allow evil imaginations to arise in your mind to find fault with this statement. Remember: our Lord Jesus Christ is the One Who freely gave the best wine to His friends at the marriage supper. He also approved of costly oil being poured over Him. And, when He was crucified, His coat was of the very best kind, motivating the soldiers to cast lots for it. In the book of Revelation, in Chapter 1, He is seen standing among the golden candlesticks wearing a girdle of solid gold.

God will supply the needs of His faithful partners to evangelize the world, *in accordance with His riches in glory!*

Lesson 76: Scripturally Giving to Your Teacher

Every Christian has some special teacher who is vital in his or her Christian life. There are prophecy teachers, Bible teachers, pastors, evangelists, and those, like me, who give instruction in the financial matters of the Word.

There is a continuous flow of good teaching available to us each day. But did you know that the Bible tells us that if we are receiving a blessing from a teacher, then we should share good things with that teacher?

> **Let him that is taught in the word communicate unto** (share with) **him that teacheth in all good things.**
>
> **Galatians 6:6**

I hope that by this time in our study, you have learned this truth. I do not bring this up because I desire a gift from you, but, like Paul, I do desire fruit that will abound to your account!

I am teaching this concept because *it is the truth,* and only as you know the truth can you be set totally free! Galatians 6:6 declares it. God says that we should take our good things and share them with those who teach His Word.

What a great plan this is. The Lord gives us great anointed teachers to bring us His wonderful Word. After we learn the Word, we go forth and benefit and prosper from that Word. Then, we share some of that prosperity with our teacher to help meet his needs and to fulfill God's Word which says: **Thou shalt not muzzle the ox when he treadeth out the corn** (Deut. 25:4). God has decreed that our teachers should eat freely from the harvest they plant in our spirits.

When you give to your teacher, you unleash God's prosperity even more powerfully in your own life. You give the heavenly Father yet another avenue through which He can bless you.

What a wonderful, ever-increasing cycle of blessing!

Now look at the very next line of that scripture in Galatians:

> **Be not deceived; God is not mocked: for whatsoever a man soweth, that shall he also reap.**
> **Galatians 6:7**

As you sow a blessing *to* your teacher, you will reap a blessing *from* your teacher and grow into an even deeper understanding of God's Word. Bless those who teach you, and God promises that He will bless you in return.

Lesson 77: Removing the Veil from Malachi 3:10

Because of the importance of this principle, I must re-emphasize it. This is one of the most important lessons in this book because it answers a much-asked question by well-intentioned Christians. "Brother John, I have been faithfully tithing now for ten years, and very frankly, I have never, even one time, received a blessing so great that there was not room enough to receive it!"

Every tithing Christian probably relates to this dilemma.

Here is why the tithe has not been manifesting the blessing described in Malachi 3:10. Most Christians are giving precisely *ten percent* and not a penny more! When you tithe, you are simply returning to God what is already His. It is not a gift, because if you keep it, you are robbing God!

The spiritual principles that govern the blessings of the tithe are contained in Malachi 3:10:

> **Bring ye all the tithes into the storehouse, that there may be meat in mine house, and prove me now herewith, saith the Lord of hosts, if I will not open you the windows of heaven, and pour you out a blessing, that *there shall* not *be room* enough *to receive it.***

I have emphasized seven words in this text that are written in italics in the *King James Version*. It is common knowledge that all italicized words in the *King James Version* have been added by the translators to the original Greek text. Here is one of the few big errors in the translation of the Authorized Version.

These words, *"there," "shall," "be," "room," "to" "receive,"* and *"it,"* are added words, which do not clarify the original text, as italicized words are supposed to do, but, in my opinion, actually add a meaning that God did not intend.

The passage should properly read: "...and pour out for you a blessing, *that not enough."**

You see, tithing only opens the windows of heaven. If you had someone living next to you who was stealing from you, you wouldn't leave the windows open.

The same is true of God. When we fail to tithe, we are stealing from Him, and *the windows of financial blessing* shut in our lives!

But, when we do tithe, God opens the windows of heaven. But remember: the literal meaning of the original text says *that is not enough.* We must then complete the process through offerings to establish the rate of return out of those windows. After we tithe to open the windows, then we put to work Luke 6:38.

The only giving we do is through our offerings, over and above the tithe. These offerings are so critical because they determine how much we receive in return from God through the open windows (opened by the tithe):

> ...For with the same measure that ye mete withal (measure), it shall be measured to you again.
>
> **Luke 6:38**

---

*Please read Malachi 3:10 in the following versions: *The Berkeley Version, The Jerusalem Bible, The Douay Version, The New English Bible,* and *Ferrar Fenton's Version.* You will find that none of these say there will be a blessing so great "that there shall not be room enough to receive it."

Remember: your tithe opens the windows of heaven, and your offering establishes the measure God will use to give back to you through the open windows.

Five Kinds of Giving
In Summary

If you want nice, simple, easy answers concerning giving and receiving, you will not find them in God's Word. You see, He has created His principles of biblical economics, and they require time, study, and understanding if they are to become effective and *powerful* in your life. The biblical principles of economics are *not an "instant" prosperity formula*. They demand understanding *and* a new relationship with God.

The gift of your salvation is given freely, but it then takes a constant daily walk to keep your relationship with God growing.

You received the Holy Spirit simply by asking, but if you plan to put all of the gifts and fruits of the Holy Spirit into *powerful practice* in your life, it takes a lifetime of interaction with Him.

The same is true of the biblical principle of giving and receiving.

It is not an instantaneous gift. The principle of giving and receiving demands careful study to understand God's will for you in this matter. It demands faithful execution in a systematic, concise manner. And then, after faith and patience have done their work, you inherit the promises. (Hebrews 6:12.)

In this section, you have seen that there are many types of giving.

I listed tithing as one method of giving to God. The tithe is a sum of God's money that has been entrusted to your keeping. Failing to give it back to Him at the proper time is absolute robbery.

But, the act of tithing is the *foundational principle of biblical economics* since the windows of heaven cannot be opened unto you until you tithe.

You learned that offerings are the key to the measure of your prosperity. Your faithful tithing opens the windows, and your faithful, liberal offerings determine how much God will bless you through the open windows. Giving only a little measure of what you have as an offering brings a little measure of blessing through the windows, but a big measure brings forth a big blessing.

Mission-giving unleashes a very special promise *just for you!* No other saints can experience prosperity in quite the same way as those who give to missions. Mission-minded saints can look forward to both quantity and quality blessings from God.

Giving is a spiritual gift which you and I learn to use by *application.* It is *not enough* for you to understand everything that I've written and shared with you in this book, and it is not enough for you to memorize every single scripture I've quoted so far, and then *stand in faith* for your prosperity. To achieve God's desired prosperity, to achieve the abundance that will give you the ability to effectively participate in the end-time harvest, *you must faithfully apply these principles* in your everyday life:

1. *Give* your gift in the name of Jesus.

2. *Pray* over your gift; consecrate it to God's service, then

3. *Release* your gift so God can unleash His *powerful principles* of abundant supply back into your life.

Give consistently. Give when it is not easy to give; give when it is joyous. Give as the poor widow who, in desperation, threw into the treasury her last two mites.

Simply stated: just *give.*

God looks at your heart, not at the dollar amount of your gift. He determines the size (or measure) of your gift by what portion it is of what you have left. If you are giving out of your need, even if it is only one cent, your one penny is a gift of more value than a million dollars given by someone else out of his great abundance!

That is the only way it can be fair, and our God is a just God. These principles make no sense to the world, but they make great sense to God, and, they are making more and more sense to you as you receive a whole new mentality on the subject of finances. Your mind is being revolutionized and renovated, and brought into line, precept upon precept, with the Word of God!

Section XI:
Who Is Behind Your Poverty?

Lesson 78: The Source of Poverty

Many people believe that poverty and prosperity are both matters of birth or luck. They believe that some people are meant to be poor and others are meant to be rich.

That is not what the Word of God says.

God has established certain *general* principles of economics that govern who will be rich and who will be poor. These principles pertain to the lost as well as the saved.

Principle 1: Laziness tends to poverty.

> **How long wilt thou sleep, O sluggard? when wilt thou arise out of thy sleep?**
>
> **Yet a little sleep, a little slumber, a little folding of the hands to sleep:**
>
> **So shall thy poverty come as one that travelleth, and thy want as an armed man.**
>
> **Proverbs 6:9-11**

The Word says if a person is lazy (and sleeps a lot) and does not work (but just sits, folding his hands, wasting time), then poverty will overtake him and will work its will in his life with the same ease and surety as a well-armed robber. A violation of the work ethic can stop the whole process of abounding in a Christian's life, even if he applies the principles discussed in this book.

If you are lazy, if you do not work, then do not expect the principles of biblical economics to work for you. Furthermore, the Word of God says you will be both poor and desperate.

Now lay hold of this truth. God will not violate His own laws. If you are lazy, you will never be able to successfully operate the principles of biblical economics described in this book. When you put two opposite forces to work in your life, they continuously hinder and nullify each other. Remember, too: your prosperity cannot come to you in appreciable measure if your laziness is keeping the armed robber of poverty in the midst of your pending harvest.

If you have a tendency toward laziness, you must change it immediately. You must defend yourself against it with the same resolution that you would defend yourself against an armed robber, remembering (amazing as it may seem) that you yourself are a big part of your problem.

We all play a great part in determining our own poverty by our actions! And, of course, Satan does his part, too. He will lie to us in every imaginable way to keep us poor. He will tell us myths about money, saying, "Money is evil; you don't need it," or he will whisper, "If you have money, it will corrupt you," or he will suggest, "You will be even poorer if you give to God," or he will declare, "It is a godly thing to be poor."

You see, poverty is a partnership. The devil wants you and me poor, and he will lie to us to keep us from doing the biblical things that will result in wealth.

Poverty is a joint venture between ourselves,

Satan, and our ignorance of God's Word. Remember: you have control over the armed robber of laziness; so rebuke it, shun it, and do not fall prey to it, for laziness will destroy the good things that God wants for you.

Lesson 79: The Source of Prosperity

Just as there are certain *general* principles of economics that lead to poverty, so too there are general principles of economics that lead to prosperity.

Principle 2: If you are not lazy and can do your work without constant supervision, then your life will tend towards prosperity.

> **Go to the ant, thou sluggard; consider her ways, and be wise:**
>
> **Which having no *guide, overseer, or ruler*,**
>
> **Provideth her meat in the summer, and gathereth her food in the harvest.**
>
> **Proverbs 6:6-8**

This is God's formula for having meat in the summer and food during the harvest. Work hard, like the ant, and do your work without requiring constant supervision! This one truth alone is part of every financial success story ever told!

A field trip to the ant hill, as the wise man of Proverbs prescribes, is absolutely essential. Whenever a hard-working, industrious man or woman puts the specific principles of biblical economics to work, all he or she does will be more effective.

God's Law of Prosperity says that if a person is a liberal giver, then his money will be increased.

When a person is industrious, he will naturally tend towards prosperity. So be careful not to lose sight of the fact that you are on a quest for the God-kind of prosperity, and it is based upon giving:

> **There is** (he) **that scattereth, and yet increaseth; and there is** (he) **that withholdeth more than is meet** (fitting), **but it tendeth to poverty.**

> *The liberal soul shall be made fat: and he that watereth shall be watered also himself.*
> **Proverbs 11:24,25**

If you put Jesus first in your finances, then *you will steadily increase* and become well-endowed in material goods.

Keep yourself in balance in your economics. Remember: there are two sets of economic principles that must be blended into any successful financial endeavor:

1. The *general* law of economics says that hard work by the person who can perform his work without supervision tends towards sufficiency.

2. The *spiritual* law of biblical economics says that when anyone gives to God, He continuously gives back to that person in ever-increasing amounts.

When you operate both the general and the spiritual laws of prosperity in your life, you will begin to experience ever-increasing abundance.

Lesson 80:
Satan Exposed...and Deposed

Satan is a thief. He is a deceptive, calculating plunderer who, if left unchecked, moves in and out of our lives at his own discretion, trying to find ways to rob and defraud us.

He has stolen the joys of family life by selling his destructive doctrine of divorce to millions of people. He has stolen the joys of sharing with others in our society by selling multiplied thousands his "me-first" philosophy.

And, he has stolen from the finances of the saints by convincing the Body of Christ that poverty is godly, and that prosperity is evil.

His lies have kept us crippled, ineffective, and impotent long enough! Satan has "ripped off" from God's children the quality of life God has intended for His saints.[1]

Establish this principle clearly in your mind. God wants you to be prosperous, and the devil wants you poor. God has given you the biblical principles of economics to achieve prosperity, and Satan has *all the lies* you need to keep you poor. Prosperity is a *material state*, but it is attained through a *spiritual battle!*

> **For we wrestle not against flesh and blood,**
> **but against principalities, against powers, against**
> **the rulers of the darkness of this world, against**
> **spiritual wickedness in high places.**
>
> **Ephesians 6:12**

It is time we expose the devil for the father of lies that he is! (John 8:44) It is time we deposed him from his position as ruler of the darkness of this world. The devil has used his lies about money to destroy good relationships, to break up families, and

---

[1] For more details read my book, *Stolen Property Returned*, which gives a step-by-step biblical process describing how to reclaim those things the devil has stolen from you. It will also show you how to keep the new wealth that is now flowing into your life through application of the principle of giving and receiving.

even to split churches. But, the money wasn't evil, it was *Satan's lies* about money that were evil!

It is time to serve notice on the devil! He has robbed you and me long enough. For too long he has "ripped off" our possessions and indiscriminately robbed the saints of God, literally diminishing our quality of life.

It is time to take a stand.

Please realize that while I have only touched on this subject in this one lesson, it is a very important issue. You see, if you do not learn how to stop the devil's robberies in your life, no matter how much you seek to prosper, you will make no real progress toward prosperity.

Lesson 81: Recognizing Your Prosperity Heritage

You now know that the devil wants you poor.

You now know that God has given you authority over the devil, and your heavenly Father wants you to abound in all good things.

By now I am sure you have rejected the old, worn-out line that says, "God is putting me through this poverty to keep me dependent upon Him." That kind of thinking belongs in the garbage can.

We are no longer talking old "pie-in-the-sky" principles, or mouthing "in the sweet by-and-by" rhetoric. We are replacing those outdated ideas with scriptural promises of our divine right to prosper here and now. Prosperity is part of our *heavenly heritage*, that which comes with being a child of the King!

With your new prosperity mentality, you are literally being transformed into a new breed of saint. You have a way to put the crooked things straight — the ability to take back what the devil has stolen. You have discovered the way to claim a significant portion of the riches of this world to use to finance the final, end-time harvest before the return of Jesus!

One passage of scripture puts into proper perspective our position in this *spiritual battle* and highlights our *spiritual heritage* better than any other:

> **Behold, *I give unto you power* to tread on serpents and scorpions, and over *all the power* of the enemy: and nothing shall by any means hurt you.**
>
> **Luke 10:19**

God has given you and me *power* over the enemy, and by now you know that poverty is clearly one of the tools the enemy has used to keep us weak and ineffective. But, we have the *power to overcome poverty*. It is part of our prosperity heritage as sons and daughters of the Most High God:

> **Forasmuch then as the children are partakers of flesh and blood, he also himself likewise took part of the same; that through death he might destroy *him that had the power* of death, that is, the devil.**
>
> **Hebrews 2:14**

Look at that carefully: the devil *had* the power, but today *he is defeated*. The devil's power to keep you sick, poor and tired has been wiped out. Now God is calling you to be a great giver and to participate in every aspect of the end-time harvest.

And, as strange as it may seem, you are now beginning to see that this wonderful truth about abundance is not just an impossible dream; it is a reality that is happening to you. You are possessing a new prosperity mentality. You are walking out of the door of financial *impossibilities* and crossing the threshold of unlimited financial *possibilities* through the power of God!

Lesson 82:
Reclaiming Your Lost Treasures

Think of how much more prosperous you would be right now if you could only reclaim those treasures in life that you've previously lost.

You may have stepped out in faith to be a missionary, only to lose your house and property in the process.

Maybe you have gone through a painful divorce and "lost everything."

Perhaps you have been the victim of alcoholism or drugs, and have been fired from your job, or even lost your home and family.

Maybe you have not been repaid the money you loaned, or perhaps the lawyer or accountant you trusted proved to be dishonest.

God, in His loving concern for you, and as part of the prosperity process, has provided you with a *spiritual way* to reclaim those lost treasures. God demands double restitution!

**If a man shall deliver unto his neighbour
money or stuff to keep, and it be stolen out of the**

man's house; *if the thief be found, let him pay double.*

Exodus 22:7

Now I know you are probably thinking:
"Brother John, that's all well and good, but I have no
idea where that crooked attorney is anymore. He has
left the state, and no one knows where he is."

Don't worry. We must focus on the true culprit
behind these robberies, no matter what was stolen.
The thief is not the dishonest lawyer, the divorce, the
liquor, the drugs. The engineer of your robbery is
Satan himself! He works in and through the children
of disobedience — unsaved men and women:

> **Wherein in time past ye walked according
> to the course of this world, according to the prince
> of the power of the air, the spirit** *that now wor-
> keth in the children of disobedience.*

Ephesians 2:2

The devil is the *true thief;* he is the one who
takes what belongs to us, whether it is our health, our
wealth, our happiness, our job, or any other of our
possessions. But, the Bible says that if we *find the
thief,* and accuse him, he must repay *double* what he
has stolen!

My friend, you and I have found the thief —
Satan himself. We are not wrestling with flesh and
blood lawyers, bankers, real estate agents, or any other person or group of people; we are wrestling with
Satan and his host of demon forces.

The next move is up to us. God is waiting for
His people to take up the *arms* He has already provided us, the *weapons of our spiritual warfare,* and take
back all that has been stolen from us.

Who Is Behind Your Poverty?
In Summary

Behind every evil activity on this earth there is a single mastermind — Satan himself. He is behind all the troubles, riots, wars, crimes, murders and thefts that have taken place in the past, and all the evil things which are *still* happening today!

When you name the true villain — Satan — in your spiritual warfare and take him to God's heavenly court, then you can begin to benefit from God's system of retribution and restoration in your life.

Peter knew how to see past the flesh and blood and go right to the source of the problem. In Acts 5:1-11, we have the example of Ananias and his wife, Sapphira. Together, they secretly devised a plot to gain prestige among their Christian brothers and sisters. They decided they could get the same recognition Barnabas received when he gave the total selling price of a piece of land to the work of God. Yet, they thought they could deceive Peter and keep a portion of the money for themselves.

But Peter saw through this lying deception and "laid the ax to the root of tree" by confronting the *real liar*:

> **But Peter said, Ananias, why hath *Satan* filled thine heart to lie...?**
>
> **Acts 5:3**

Peter knew who the real culprit was — Satan — and boldly took him to the heavenly courtroom of God. As a result, both Ananias and Sapphira received immediate judgment for allowing the enemy of God to operate through them.

Remember: the devil is the root of all sin (lies, theft, hatred, deception, etc.), but Jesus is the root of all righteousness. Your environment is not able to keep you from prospering when you follow God's laws of biblical economics.

If you are in poverty, it is not because of some chance of birth, education, ethnic origin, or whatever you think is holding you back.

Your battle and problems are with the devil and with yourself. If God has given you the *power* to get wealth, then it logically follows that Satan holds the power to bring you to poverty.

To begin now to live a prosperous life, start challenging the real sources of your problems — the devil and your own inconsistencies, even your own laziness. *Accuse* the devil in God's heavenly court. Demand your goods back. Rebuke Satan. Expel him from your thinking patterns; think only on the things God says in His Word concerning you and your prosperity.

Be strong-handed when dealing with the devil and if you can see any traces of laziness in you, purge them out of your life with the same violence and energy you use against Satan!

Poverty cannot live in you when you destroy its root causes.

Section XII:
Seven Final Steps to Prosperity!

Lesson 83: Step 1
— Give, Expecting to Receive

No matter how well you understand the principles of biblical economics discussed in this book, understanding alone is not enough to unleash God's prosperity in your life.

Contrary to common belief, the Bible does not simply say, "The truth will set you free"! John 8:32 does, however, say: **...ye shall *know* the truth, and the truth shall make you free** (John 8:32). The Greek word translated *know* goes beyond the most common usage of the English word *know.* Here, in this context, it refers to a knowing which is beyond head knowledge. It speaks of a person who actually is walking in the truth, one who is being set free by the truth he knows and practices.

At this point of our study, you no doubt understand that giving is the first step toward God's abundance in your life. You *know* that this is not achieved by just "knowing" words, but through your actual giving. (If you still do not have a strong conviction that these principles work, I suggest you go back about twenty lessons and take another look at each of these biblical precepts).

God's greatest act of giving was done with full expectation of receiving something in return. Our

Creator gave His most precious Son, Jesus Christ, to die because He knew He would receive in return sons and daughters:

> For God so loved the world, that he gave his
> only begotten Son, that whosoever believeth in
> him should not perish, but have everlasting life.
>
> John 3:16

I hope you have already planted a liberal field of money-seeds "in the name of Jesus." Now, expect to reap a money harvest from each and every seed you planted.

Some would say, "But, Brother John, that just doesn't sit well with me. When I give to God, I don't expect anything in return."

Whether you expect it or not, God will not change His laws. You give money seeds, and you will reap a money harvest. Sow deeds of kindness, and you will reap deeds of kindness, because the Bible clearly states that we get back what we give:

> Be not deceived; God is not mocked, for
> whatsoever a man soweth, that shall he also reap.
>
> Galatians 6:7

So, if you have believed God's Word and planted money seeds, *keep on believing* God's Word that you will receive a money harvest! The Bible clearly states that we will reap if we don't give up:

> And let us not be weary in well doing: for
> in due season we shall reap, if we faint not.
>
> Galatians 6:9

Isn't that wonderful? You can give, expecting a harvest! Since you can expect a harvest, while you are awaiting the return on your sowing you can be planning the strategic planting of even more money seeds from your coming money harvest. Think of it! You can have a perpetual harvest, if you have faith for perpetual seeding.

Remember: seed time and harvest are guaranteed in God's Word.

Lesson 84: Step 2
— Bank on God's Promises

Every day you and I see and hear the various commercial banks waging economic war with their competitors. They buy advertising time on radio, television, and in the newspapers, trying to offer us the right promise to get us to deposit our money in their bank.

Some offer higher interest.

Others offer no service charge on checking accounts.

Still others offer toasters, cookbooks, and yes, even Cabbage Patch dolls — just to lure us into investing our funds in their institution.

But, without exception, God offers you and me the best banking program ever heard of. Hear how attractive it sounds from *The Living Bible:*

> **But remember this — if you give little, you will get little. A farmer who plants just a few seeds will get only a small crop, but if he plants much, he will reap much.**
>
> **Every one must make up his own mind as to how much he should give. Don't force anyone to give more than he really wants to, for cheerful givers are the ones God prizes.**

219

> *God is able to make it up to you by giving you everything you need and more, so that there will not only be enough for your own needs, but plenty left over to give joyfully to others.*
>
> It is as the Scriptures say: "The godly man gives generously to the poor. His good deeds will be an honor to him forever."
>
> For God, who gives seed to the farmer to plant, and later on, good crops to harvest and eat, *will give you more and more seed to plant and will make it grow so that you can give away more and more fruit from your harvest.*
>
> *Yes, God will give you much so that you can give away much....*
>
> 2 Corinthians 9:6-11 TLB

Now that you are putting your money in God's bank, you can expect to receive God's promises which assure you of provision of everything you need and more.

You literally cannot give away too much money when you give in the name of the Lord. Each time you give an offering, it will be returned to you, multiplied. Just as an earthly banker knows the world's secrets of abundance, you can literally *bank* on God, and on His promises. He will see that you have abundant treasures in heaven and on the earth (even more than enough).

Lesson 85: Step 3
— Choose Faith Over Fear

The only way the devil can stop you from receiving your God-ordained portion of wealth is by getting you to accept his deceptive, destructive lies about your inability to break through into abundance.

He will try to make you so fearful of failing, you will give up your new-found liberty in giving.

Satan will desperately attempt to convince you that giving is foolish. This deception is rooted in fear. The devil will desperately try to put fear-filled lies into your mind, hoping they will grow like weeds and destroy your much-desired harvest.

Do not be confused as to the origin of fear; it does not come from God:

> **For God hath not given us the spirit of fear;**
> **but of *power*, and of love, and of a sound mind.**
> **2 Timothy 1:7**

God does not want you to operate in fear, but in *power*. Remember God's heritage for you as described in Deuteronomy 8:18:

> **But thou shalt remember the Lord thy God:**
> **for it is he that giveth thee *power* to get wealth....**

You see, God not only gives you *power* over fear, He also freely gives you the *power* to get wealth! What a loving God we serve!

God's way to counteract Satan's relentless, *fearful* lies about your finances, is to have you walk in *faith*. Faith and fear cannot operate together. Neither can faith and doubt. They work against each other and bring about instability and failure.

James tells us, **A double minded man is unstable in all his ways** (James 1:8). Reject fear. Reject doubt. Use each step of faith as a way of destroying Satan's attempts to bring poverty into your life. Faith will always conquer fear when it is operated in the light of biblical truth.

Remember: as you become faithful in your finances, you begin to draw a double reward to yourself.

1. You begin to prosper in the financial realm.

2. You position yourself to be endowed with the true riches of God (spiritual power and authority).

> **If therefore ye have not been faithful in the unrighteous mammon, who will commit to your trust the true riches?**
>
> **Luke 16:11**

Surely you can now see that through your *faith* in God's promises, and your faithful stewardship walk, you will become like the workers in the temple who could be trusted with finances:

> **Howbeit there was no reckoning made with them of the money that was delivered into their hand,** *because they dealt faithfully.*
>
> **2 Kings 22:7**

Lesson 86: Step 4 — Tithe and Give Offerings

It should now be firmly rooted in your spirit that God expects you to tithe and give offerings, and you are undoubtedly now faithfully performing both spiritual actions in your life. It is important for you to remember at all times that God does not ask you to give your tithes and offering to make you poor!

You are tithing to open the windows of heaven.

You are giving offerings so that God will pour out a blessing through the open windows — a blessing that is being measured back to you with the same measure that you have measured it out to Him.

Do not let down in either of these dimensions of giving. Both are necessary for you to make the major spiritual breakthrough in your finances that you so desire.

Both of these actions trigger different sets of promises from God, and each of these promises comes to you with God's strong desire to see them accomplished:

> **For all the promises of God in him are yea,**
> **and in him Amen, unto the glory of God by us.**
> **2 Corinthians 1:20**

All the promises of God are "yes"! Everything God has promised for your life, He will deliver to you. If you meet His conditions, these promises, combined with your faithful seed-faith planting, become the basis for your financial prosperity.

Your tithes and offerings are to give to God, that's true, but they are also the physical actions which release God's abundance into your life from His heavenly storehouse. So continue to faithfully give your tithes and offerings to the Lord, and then *stand in faith*, confidently expecting God's promises to be fulfilled in your life.

Don't let it make a difference in your giving plan if you do not see a sudden increase in your checkbook balance. Don't let it change your plan, even if your budget remains tight for a while, or even if your electric bill doubles, or two car tires blow out at the same time.

No matter what the circumstances, the tithing and offering process you are now undertaking will be the tool God uses to unleash His financial abundance in your life. And, in time, there will no longer be a wilderness in your finances, but your desert will bloom like a beautiful garden.

This will not happen because I say so — it will happen because the Word of God says so!

Remember the old saying: "God said it, I believe it, that settles it!"

Add to that saying: "When I do it, my actions make it happen to me!"

Lesson 87: Step 5
— Plant Your Seed to Glorify God

The biblical principles of economics are now firmly rooted in your mind and (hopefully) in your actions. The Lord's method of seed planting and sowing shatters much of the world's thinking. The world teaches:

1. "Get all you can (get every cent you can)."

2. "Can all you get (save every penny you get)."

3. "Sit on the can (never spend any of your savings)."

In other words: "Get all you can, and *hold it.*"

But God has a different way:

> There is (he) that scattereth, and yet increaseth; and there is (he) that withholdeth more than is meet (fitting), but it tendeth to poverty.

> The liberal soul shall be made fat: and he that watereth shall be watered also himself.
> **Proverbs 11:24,25**

You have planted your seeds with a cheerful attitude and a good heart in order to glorify God. Now you can expect an abundant harvest. Because you have been generous in your seed planting, God guarantees that you will be prospered, made "fat" (with goods), watered and blessed.

That's His promise to you.

When the devil starts to feed you his lies of fear and pending shortage, remember to "cast down" these evil "imaginations." And once again stand on the promises of God. You have seen them repeated again and again on the pages of this book, because God says repetition is good for us, and He has created our minds to learn things precept upon precept, line upon line.

Remember: you live in a constant barrage of the devil's false precepts every day of your life. While you might not clearly see them as lies, their total overall effect is strong. They make a strong impression on your subconscious mind. So in this book I have tried to give equal time to God's truths.

> **Be not deceived; God is not mocked: for whatsoever a man soweth, that shall he also reap.**
> **Galatians 6:7**

I have sown biblical seeds of prosperity into your mind, and now that you are planting your financial crop, you will, upon the authority of God's Word, soon be reaping an ever-increasing harvest so you can have everything you need and plenty left over to effectively finance His end-time harvest:

> **God is able to make it up to you by giving you everything you need and more, so that there**

will not only be enough for your own needs, but
plenty left over to give joyfully to others.

2 Corinthians 9:8 TLB

Lesson 88: Step 6
— Reap Your Harvest

The circumstances in your life may not show
any sudden changes. Your finances may still be tight.
The bills may still be difficult to pay. You probably do
not yet fully see God's blessings in such great abundance in your life that your every need and want is
being met.

But, stand on God's promises. You are tithing to
keep the windows of heaven open, and you are giving offerings to establish a healthy, abundant flow
through those windows.

How many Christians have you heard say:
"Can you help me? I don't *feel* saved"?

They have believed the words of salvation, they
accepted Jesus, but somewhere in their walk they let
Satan's lies temporarily cause them to doubt. Now
they are seeking for assurance from others that they
are truly saved.

"Well," they say, "maybe I should repeat John
3:16 and the sinner's prayer again, just to be sure."

Have you ever heard that? Has anyone ever
said it to you? It shows that someone has been listen-
ing to the lies of the devil concerning salvation.

Well, get ready. Satan will probably throw some
stupid lies at you concerning your soon-coming harvest. He will lie and say something like this: "You
gave that big offering last week, and what did it get

you? You still don't have anything. This is all just a great big 'rip-off.'"

Stop thinking that before you end up in the poorhouse.

Learn to recognize these lies, and cast them out of your mind.

Do not give attention to anything that exalts itself against the knowledge of God. These fear tactics are the only means the devil has to try and stop your pending financial harvest.

You gave according to God's word, and you *will reap* a harvest according to God's Word. As sure as God's Word is true (and we know it is), your harvest is even now beginning to manifest itself.

Remember: the Word of God guarantees your harvest. Think about it. When the United States government guarantees the price of a crop, the farmers plant all their fields, faithfully trusting the government to keep its promise to provide them a fair price for their harvest.

How much more can the sons and daughters of God trust Him and plant with confidence, knowing that He will provide us the harvest He has promised.

Sow your seeds in faith and trust the God of Faith to deliver the promised harvest.

Lesson 89: Step 7
— Always Replant a Portion
of Every Harvest You Reap!

As your financial harvest starts manifesting itself in your life, it isn't always immediately identifiable. Remember that years of traditional thinking have made it easy for you to mistakingly think of the bank or maybe your job or material investments as being your source.

Keep your eyes open. Watch for God's blessings, since they may come without clearly being recognized as your much-awaited harvest from God for seeds you planted months ago!

You may catch yourself saying: "Boy, my business is going great lately," or "Hey, my boss just gave me an unexpected raise," or "Man, that new bank did some marvelous things with my investments."

Part of your continuing success process in effectively applying God's laws of biblical economics is dependent upon your recognition of the fact that God is your Source. It is God Who supplies all the needs of His children.

With every upward advance in your finances, learn to say: "Thank You, Lord. I recognize this increase as part of your blessing process which my scriptural giving has released in my life. I give You the honor and the glory for the abundant harvest You are now manifesting in my financial matters."

When you recognize the Source of your every blessing, then you will recognize your need to continue with the next step — the replanting of some of every increase into the fields of God for the *next harvest*.

If the devil first fails in his attempts to stop you from giving by putting strong doubts about God's promises in your mind, his second deception is even more subtle. He simply tries to cloud the Source of the increases in your funds, so you will forget to plant new seeds from your abundance. He knows that you will plant if you remember that God is the Source of your blessings, so he attempts to distract you with lies about your boss or your bank or even your own business dealings really being your source.

Simply tithe and give generous offerings on all income you receive: your income tax refunds, extra income, virtually any money you receive. Don't allow any room for discretion or doubt.

If a stranger comes up and hands you a ten-dollar bill, thank the Lord, tithe a dollar, and give a portion away in an offering to God.

Cast down evil imaginations that creep in and push the Spirit of God aside. Keep planting from every harvest.

Remember: the paramount truth is that you must plant with regularity if you wish to reap with regularity.

Lesson 90: Let Me Hear From You!

I am excited for you, and for the Kingdom of God.

I know this book has touched your life, or you would not be reading this final segment. You have dared to believe God's Word enough to read this far, and I am sure you have already put these principles of biblical economics to work in your life.

So I'm excited. God's excited. And I'm sure you're excited.

When God does pour out blessings on your life — and He will — please write to me and share the good news, the victory reports. I want to hear about the marvelous blessings God is providing in your life. Send me pictures of your new car, let me see your new home, tell me about the college to which you are now able to send your son or daughter. Most importantly, *share with me the various ministry outreaches, and the mighty spiritual projects you have been able to help or launch — with your new financial harvest.*

God cares about you, and so do I. You see, I didn't write this book for my benefit; I wrote it for yours. So now, take a few moments and write back to me and share what God is doing in your life.

God bless you abundantly as you continue to develop these powerful truths that will enable you to be an effective part in financing the end-time harvest — God's way!

John Avanzini was born in Paramaribo, Surinam, South America, in 1936. He was raised and educated in Texas, and received his doctorate in philosophy from Baptist Christian University, Shreveport, Louisiana. Dr. Avanzini now resides with his wife, Pat, in Fort Worth, Texas, where he is the Director of His Image Ministries.

Dr. Avanzini's television program, *Principles of Biblical Economics*, is aired five times per day, seven days per week, by more than 550 television stations from coast to coast. He speaks nationally and internationally in conferences and seminars every week. His tape and book ministry is worldwide, and many of his vibrant teachings are now available in tape and book form.

Dr. Avanzini is an extraordinary teacher of the Word of God, bringing forth many of the present truths that God is using in these days to prepare the Body of Christ for His triumphant return.

To contact Dr. Avanzini, write:

John Avanzini
P.O. Box 1057
Hurst, Texas 76053

*Please include your prayer requests
and comments when you write.*

Other Books by John Avanzini

Always Abounding

Faith Extenders

30-60-Hundredfold

Rapid Debt-Reduction Strategies

Stolen Property Returned

War On Debt

The Wealth of the World

**Available from
your local bookstore,
or from**

HARRISON HOUSE
P.O. Box 35035
Tulsa, OK 74153